30-minute RUBBER STAMP WORKSHOP

Sandra McCall

NORTH LIGHT BOOKS

CINCINNATI, OHIO

www.artistsnetwork.com

metric conversion chart

TO CONVERT	TO	MULTIPLY BY
Inches	Centimeters	2.54
Centimeters	Inches	0.4
Feet	Centimeters	30.5
Centimeters	Feet	0.03
Yards	Meters	0.9
Meters	Yards	1.1
Sq. Inches	Sq. Centimeters	6.45
Sq. Centimeters	Sq. Inches	0.16
Sq. Feet	Sq. Meters	0.09
Sq. Meters	Sq. Feet	10.8
Sq. Yards	Sq. Meters	0.8
Sq. Meters	Sq. Yards	1.2
Pounds	Kilograms	0.45
Kilograms	Pounds	2.2
Ounces	Grams	28.4
Grams	Ounces	0.04

Other fine North Light Books are available from your local bookstore or art supply store or direct from the publisher.

06 05 04 03 02   5 4 3 2 1
Library of Congress Cataloging-in-Publication Data
McCall, Sandra.
30-minute rubber stamp workshop / by Sandra McCall.
  p. cm.
Includes index.
ISBN 1-58180-271-4 (pbk. : alk. paper)
1. Rubber stamp printing. I. Title.
TT867 .M34 2002
761–dc21

                        2002026305

Editors: Jane Friedman and Jolie Lamping Roth
Designer: Stephanie Strang
Layout artist: Kathy Gardner
Production coordinator: Sara Dumford
Photographers: Tim Grondin, Al Parrish and Christine Polomsky

acknowledgments

For the crew at North Light, thank you, thank you, thank you! To my editor, Jane Friedman; photographer, Christine Polomsky; sales manager, Sally Finnegan; and Executive Editor Tricia Waddell, a big, huge hug. You are all very special people who know how to help without being intrusive and THAT takes talent!

Thanks to my brothers, sisters, friends and students with the light hearts and sense of silly fun. You make it easy.

Continued thanks goes to my two greatest cheerleaders—my mom, Betty Cox Griffiths, and my mother-in-law, Connie Hernandez. I love you both.

A special thanks goes to Linda T. at Clearsnap, Lay at Hero Arts, Karen at JudiKins, Glenda at Plaid, Kari at The Leather Factory, Kathy at Postmodern Design and Audrey at Stamp Oasis. I appreciate your generous support.

Finally, there is one little reader whose name I did not catch in the frantic hubbub of the Glendale, Arizona, show of 2001. It's my hope that she is reading this book and will know how important she is to me. She bravely came forward, expressed her appreciation of my first book and asked if the next book would have easier gifts that she could make for her friends. Well, Little One, this book is because of you, too. I wish you and your friends many happy, art-filled days ahead.

About the AUTHOR

A freelance artist living in southern California with her husband, Les Gains, Sandra enjoys finding new ways to marry basic art supplies and stamp-related products. Her primary interests include art bookbinding, surface embellishment on both paper and fabric, collage and multi-medium assemblage.

Sandra has written several successful how-to articles for *Somerset Studio*, *National Stampagraphic* and *The Rubber Stamper*. *RubberStampMadness* profiled Sandra and her techniques in the October 1999 issue. Sandra has made guest appearances on the *Carol Duvall Show* to further promote the art of rubber stamping. Her first book, *Making Gifts with Rubber Stamps*, published by North Light Books, is available in stamp and bookstores nationwide.

photograph by Les Gains

dedication

I would like to dedicate this book to my husband,

LES GAINS.

He is my ever-changing source of laughter, surprise, inspiration and curiosity. My partner in crime and creativity, he is my best friend.

Les, I love you with all my heart.

table of CONTENTS

INTROduction

MY first book, *Making Gifts With Rubber Stamps,* continues to receive wonderful comments from enthusiastic readers. As great as the comments are, a couple of important points keep coming up in the conversations: "All the projects are so beautiful, but I never have the time to make anything that takes longer than an hour to complete," and "I can't afford to go out and buy all those supplies."

I completely understand the time and money constraints that so many of us are under today. If you have taken stamp art classes, then you know the typical class lasts around two hours. Even with all my precutting and prep work, we are pressed to finish the projects in that amount of time. I like to go into detail, make the chipboard forms rather than purchase them, and pour on layers and layers of texture. This book forced me to keep the projects simple and quick but with that funky, artsy quality. All of these projects use inexpensive materials too. What a fun challenge!

Now, as simple and quick as these projects are, I have to insert a disclaimer here. The time factors are based on the premise that your materials and colors have already been chosen. If you are like me, you take four hours to make a color decision and then an hour to complete the project. To make projects go faster, choose color combi-

nations that you already know and love to work with or work with the colors shown in the samples. Needing a quick gift is not the time to experiment with color choices. The same goes for materials—use what you have on hand and forget the exotic materials that will require a lot of searching during a shopping trip.

You can eat up a lot of time in the planning stages too, so keep it simple. I'll let you in on some tips throughout the book that will make your crafts quicker and easier to do, so keep an eye out for the additional notes and the time-saver icon . This 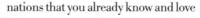 icon means the step is optional. You can skip it to save time!

All of the techniques used in this book look equally attractive whether you use them on paper, fabric, leather, wood or metal. The ideas can be translated to any number of crafts so, throughout your day, think, think, think. Get creative and make

do with what you have, what you find on the ground, or what you can trade or buy inexpensively in bargain and craft stores.

One last thing: I have included specific product names in most of the materials lists. I experiment a lot and am always looking for the best product. I've listed most of my favorite products. They definitely work and will give you great results.

Some of the products in the materials lists are optional. For instance, foil and glue work just as well as the hot foil pen, and a paintbrush and a cup of water work just as well as a JudiKins water brush—the optional materials are just fun to use.

Part of teaching is to give you the benefit of my experiments. I want to expose you to a variety of products and show you how fun they are to work with. Of course, you should always experiment on your own. You may already know about or will find a product that you like better. New products come along every day, so never give up the search for the better way.

BASIC TOOLS and SUPPLIES

The next few pages cover the general tools and supplies used in rubber stamping. Some of my favorite brands are given as examples in case you need guidance. Most likely you already have your favorite brands, too!

◎ Stamps

Generally, the deeper the etching on a rubber stamp, the better quality it is. A deeper image will allow better depth for stamping on clay, a better impression for stamping on fabric, and will stand up to more abuse.

Choose different stamps for different projects. For instance, you will want a bold image and a deeply etched stamp for stamping in clay or for doing monoprints rather than a very detailed image.

You can purchase unmounted stamps (only the rubber image, no wood or cushion) through the mail, at conventions or at some rubber stamp stores. Unmounted stamps can be stored in 3-ring binders in pocket holders or on sheet protectors. There is a variety of mounting methods for unmounted stamps. I often use double-stick tape between a block of acrylic and the unmounted stamp. If a large unmounted stamp will not stamp clearly, you can add a cushion by attaching a layer of fun foam to the back of the unmounted stamp with rubber cement. Other practical cushions would be a terry face cloth, or something soft, such as a computer mouse pad, placed under the paper to be stamped.

◎ Heat gun

My favorite is the Milwaukee. It melts embossing powder fast and it's inexpensive. It does have a strong airstream though, so you may want to get one of the smaller guns with a lower temperature and lower air force. The smaller guns work well to shrink plastic and emboss things into your powder like glitter stars and other lightweight things you don't want blown off the table. Speaking of lightweight things, when you have to emboss something small or you are shrinking a piece of plastic,

you may want to set the item into a small shallow box to keep it from flying off the table. It's also helpful to start the gun right over the object to capture it in the airflow. Starting the gun first and then moving it onto the object will definitely push it out of position.

◎ Cutting mat

I like the white Staedtler mat because it is easy to see the lines no matter what color my working materials are. I made the mistake of buying a dark mat when I first started crafting and quickly found that if I was working with a dark cardstock, it was hard to line up my paper edges with the grid lines of the mat. Also, you can lay your mat over a lightbox and see through it for pattern cutting.

◎ Straightedge

Buy a good metal ruler in a length that will accommodate most of your projects. A useful length for me is the 15″ (38cm) ruler. The cork backing will keep the ruler from slipping over your work. It also raises the metal surface off the paper so that if you use a marker along it, the ink will not bleed under the ruler making a marred line.

◎ Shrink plastic

Shrink plastic is fun to work with for a variety of reasons. You can learn to work with it easily, and it lends itself to lots of applications. I consider it to be unexplored territory and, therefore, wide open for your discoveries and radical new techniques. Available in black, brown, clear, semi-opaque, white and ivory, you can buy shrink plastic from Nasco, Lucky Squirrel, Suze Weinberg and most stamp stores.

Papers

A variety of papers are used in the projects. They include:

- *Chipboard.* This is just that stuff you find on the back of writing tablets, cereal boxes and the like. You probably already have lots of it at home, but if you need to buy some, a paper store such as Kelly Paper (see the Resources section on page 122) will carry it (you may have to order the thicker type), and some framing stores also stock it, as do some craft stores.

- *Corrugated cardboard.* It differs from chipboard in that it is the heavy rippled craft paper sandwiched in between two layers of heavy craft paper.

- *Cardstock.* This is the catchall phrase for heavier papers that you use to make greeting cards. This type of paper will range from the lighter weight "index" to medium weight "card," with the heaviest weight being "cover" stock. Any of these weights will work for cards and the projects in this book.

- *Pads of Paper.* You can make pads of paper with padding compound (see Quick Notepads on pages 41-42), using whatever size and material you want. On the other hand, you can buy pads of paper and skip making your own.

- *Mulberry paper or tissue.* You can find it in just about any stamp store, craft store or specialty paper store.

- *Calculator tape.* This is available through any office supply store. I love it for little accordion fold books because I do not have to measure and cut what seem to be endless strips of paper for my text blocks. Now if only they would make it in lots of different colors and widths!

Fabrics

PLAIN MUSLIN, or any smooth cotton fabric, welcomes your stamp art and is easy to glue together. A synthetic fabric may be harder to glue because it wants to bounce up, and you will have to hold it until the glue has set. A synthetic fabric may also resist dyes and paints that are watered down.

FELT makes excellent disposable stamp pads, great padding material and great stuffing. It also looks cool as a final surface on which to embellish with beads and embroidery work. Available in several colors, weights and sizes (by the yard or the square), felt is found in fabric and craft stores.

PRE-PRINTED FABRIC will serve you well when you are short on time. There are several very pretty batiks on the market—some of which are light enough for you to add your own color and stamp work. As with muslin, remember to buy cotton fabric for ease of use with glues and coloring materials.

FUSIBLE WEBBING (used in the Fabric Notebook Cover project on pages 34-37) can be used to fuse layers of paper and chipboard as well as fabric. It makes a great glue and can stiffen or add body to a project. Interfacings are also available as an iron-fusible material.

INKS and INKPADS

◉ Pigment ink

Pigment inkpads stay wet longer and are for stamping, embossing and coloring directly onto paper. The ink will not dry well on a slick surface and must be embossed. Mat paper will take pigment very well and have no problem drying if you don't put the ink on too thick. Pigment inks work on fabric and can be embossed or left as is. Petal Point and Crafter's from Clearsnap are examples of pigment ink.

Top Boss embossing stamp pad is a **CLEAR PIGMENT INKPAD** used for embossing items when you don't want or need any ink color. You would use this to tap clear ink onto surfaces when you want to add a coat of clear embossing powder. It's also useful for coating the rubber stamp so that it won't stick where you want an intaglio effect on shrink plastic or hot, thick embossing powder.

◉ Dye inkpads

Dye inkpads come in many, many colors and are for direct stamping and coloring of paper. They are extremely vivid when stamped on white gloss cardstock, and they dry quickly without having to be embossed. Clearsnap's Vivid mini pads make great designs when applied directly to the paper. You can press the whole pad down to make cool rectangles, you can press the corners of the pads for cute little triangles, or lay the edge of the pad down for neat stripes. These mini pads are one of my favorite tools for decorating paper, with or without stamps.

◉ Waterproof inkpad

Ancient Page acid-free, archival, waterproof dye inkpads are my favorite permanent inkpad. Some permanent inkpads need a couple minutes to dry before you can actually watercolor over the stamped image, but the Ancient Page ink dries extremely fast and you can wet it almost as soon as you stamp it. Ancient Page works great on shrink plastic too, but be careful before you shrink, as it will not dry until heated.

◉ Permanent ink

The dye inkpads that are waterproof will bead up on plastic and metal, so you will want to get an ink that is for nonporous surfaces. Permanent inks are known for their permanence, intense smell and the fact that you have to use a solvent-based cleaner to clean the stamps. This ink will dye your stamps as well as everything else, so do be careful. Wear only your craft clothes when you use this ink. The products that are used for stamping in the home (on tiles for instance), such as Zim or Décor-It, are examples of these types of inks.

You will want a piece of felt on a plastic plate or a piece of chipboard with aluminum foil next to the permanent ink. This will be your inkpad. You can buy pads for permanent inks but foil or felt works fine.

◉ Clean up

JudiKins Fabric & Permanent Ink Cleaner is among my favorites for cleaning stamps. It gets just about anything off rubber stamps, and I can use it on my tabletop or wherever I may have spilled ink.

COLOR APPLICATORS

For as many artists as there are in the world, there are probably as many color applicators. My favorite applicators are still my fingers, but there are a few times when they just will not do. Here are a few of my other favorites that are used in this book. Most of the items pictured are readily available through stamp stores, craft stores or the Internet.

Color Dusters

Resembling little shaving brushes, these are the brainchild of and distributed by JudiKins. You can use them wet like a paintbrush or dry like a stipple brush. I suggest using one duster per color family on your inkpads and one per color family with your paints. For instance, use one for the yellows, one for the reds and so on. That way, you will not have to rinse them out (except when using wet acrylic paint) and they will not corrupt your inkpads. Inexpensive enough to buy several at a time, Color Dusters will give a wide range of textures to your artwork.

Regarding stippling: If you want a cool, splotchy texture, load the duster from a wet inkpad and dab directly onto your artwork using a light or heavy touch as your desired outcome dictates. If you want a soft, smooth look, then load the duster, stipple off excess color onto scratch paper and then stipple the image. As with most color applications, start light and work layers to add depth of color.

Hot foil pen

This pen from Staedtler works with a battery and makes it possible to add foil to just about any surface without the mess of foiling adhesives. I have used it in this book as a fun, quick and easy method of foiling. Keep in mind that there are times when you will want the foil and glue as well. Plaid makes an excellent Dimensional Foiling Adhesive for the projects where you want a lot of texture and you can take a little more time to finish them.

Foam brushes

These brushes are inexpensive and valuable for several applications, the most obvious being to paint directly. They make great glue applicators for découpage. I also find them to be excellent inkpads when I want to stamp with acrylic paint.

To make your inkpad from a foam brush, squeeze a little bit of acrylic on a plate and dab the brush onto the paint, inking only one side of the foam. Then you can use the brush to ink your stamp. To get a good impression, you must tap lightly and try not to get too much paint down in the valleys of the stamp. If you do, wipe the paint off and start over. Do not rub the brush across the stamp because that only causes more paint to get in the depressions and rubs it off the stamp surface. This applies to regular inkpads as well.

Other useful applicators are a sea sponge for both paint and inkpads, a stencil brush, paintbrushes in a variety of sizes and materials, a blending pen for brush markers and a spray bottle for splatters.

PAINTS, PENS and PENCILS

of the same properties. It is a water-clean-up paint, easy to use, and permanent on slick surfaces after a 72-hour cure time. It is permanent on fabric, stays softer than acrylics and requires no heat setting. Try it on shrink plastic—the results are intriguing and quite beautiful.

Pens and pencils

These are my favorite coloring tools—the ones that have a permanent home on my desktop, the ones that I could not possibly live without.

- *Staedtler's watercolor crayons*
- *JudiKins water brush*
- *Berol Prismacolor pencils*

- *Oil-based paint marker (Painty Metallic)*
- *Krylon's 18kt Gold Leafing Pen*
- *Uniball Vision Permanent ink pen*
- *Emboss Dual Pen II from Tsukineko*
- *Staedtler Mars Graphic 3000 duo-tipped brush markers*
- *Staedtler gel roller*
- *black Sharpie*
- *chalks and glitter pens*

Paints

PLAID'S FOLKART METALLIC PAINT is probably my most used paint product. Both the metallic and the Apple Barrel craft paints come in a variety of colors and they work for most projects. Use a foam brush to apply the acrylic to your stamps as described in the Color Applicators section on page 11.

LUNA LIGHTS INK from Stamp Oasis is not an acrylic paint, though it shares many

GLAZES and RICH FINISHES

⊙ Glazes

TREASURE CRYSTAL COTE from Plaid is my favorite glaze. It gives the most wonderful, glossy shine with just one coat. All of this takes only one little disposable brush and you have no hassle with mixing a two-part resin. It will dry to the touch in about twenty minutes but will take about twenty-four hours to cure. Also, it will run solvent-based inks, so you may have to set them with a spray sealant before you apply the Crystal Cote.

For quicker results, water clean up and a great shine, I like **JUDIKINS DIAMOND GLAZE.** If you apply a very light coat, it will take about ten minutes to dry and give a good shine. Add another coat, let dry and the shine will deepen. Continue in this manner until you have the depth that you like. Remember, several light coats will dry faster than one thick application; also, a thick application will dry with a milky cast, so be patient.

FIEBING'S LEATHER SHEEN is a spray sealant. It will deepen the art colors and add a nice patina to the leather. It also makes it easier to wipe the leather clean during later use.

⊙ Beads

You will want an assortment of beads—some to sew, some to thread onto wire for dangles, some to glue and some to add to the embossing powders and the glazes. Gold beads add a rich texture to just about anything.

The tiny holeless beads from JudiKins are available in silver and gold as well as some great anodized colors. In this book I used them as a sparkling addition to embossing powders (see the Beautiful Bookends project on pages 23-26), but they can also be glued directly to your projects (see Leather Band project on pages 88-91).

For a fine line of tiny beads, use a toothpick to apply glue to the project, lay it in a box top, sprinkle the beads onto the glue and let it dry. After the glue has dried, you can tap the excess beads off the project and return them to the bottle.

⊙ Roxs

Roxs come in several anodized colors and are the product of JudiKins. As the name implies, they look and have the texture of tiny little rocks. Like the tiny beads, Roxs can be embossed or glued to your projects and will add a touch of pizzazz to your work.

⊙ Embossing powders

You can buy embossing powders from stamp stores. They are a thermographic powder that come in a variety of colors and textures. You will want a heat gun to melt the embossing powder. An iron, a light bulb or a hair dryer will work eventually, but, trust me, you won't want to spend the time with these slow methods of melting powder.

JudiKins Amazing Glaze is a thick embossing powder that I used in several projects in this book.

SMALL TOOLS and SAFETY

⊙ Pin vise

This is a handle with different sized chucks to hold a variety of small drill bits. You can easily drill through anything simply by turning the pin vise like it's a screwdriver. I use it on chipboard, polymer clay, paper clay, and to drill out beads that need a bigger hole. Pin vises are available at hobby shops.

⊙ Awl

Use it for punching holes into items such as chipboard, leather or a stack of papers to be stab bound.

⊙ Pliers

Get a pair of small needle-nose pliers with a cutter on it to help with the wire shaping and cutting.

⊙ Assorted files

Use them to smooth the edges of cut metal.

⊙ Wood rasp set

Use a wood rasp set to file and sand rough edges, even on metal.

⊙ Work gloves and mask

These are a must if you are cutting any sharp metal and/or burning it. *Do* wear a mask whenever you burn metal that has lacquer on it, while sanding or whenever airborne particles are present. Take the care of your lungs seriously! And while we are on the subject of safety, several of the glues used in this book are flammable and are toxic to breathe—some even fatal to swallow. Please use the prescribed precautions, work in a well-ventilated area and use a fan to blow the fumes away from your face and out the window, if possible.

PLIERS

PIN VISES

AWL

ASSORTED FILES

CARVING and FINE TOOLS

Carving supplies

Pictured at the right are two hand-carved stamps, an artist carving block and carving gouge.

The Staedtler artist's carving block is so easy to carve that you don't even need a blade. You can get fast and great designs by using any available tool to cut, gouge, scrape and poke into the material. For instance, a Phillips head screwdriver makes excellent little stars, a pencil makes great circles, and a fork makes neat little dots in a row.

Stylus

Use it to score paper and for dry-embossing.

Crochet and knitting needles

I use it to wrap wire for coils. A knitting needle also works great as a mandrel and both come in a variety of sizes.

Bone folder

Those who know me will laugh that this is in a tools picture. Everyone knows that I do not own a bone folder, but it is, of course, useful for scoring and folding paper.

Tweezers

It is useful for picking up small items like tiny beads. Another option that I have started using in place of tweezers is a toothpick with a tiny ball of tacky glue on the end. I make it so that it is just tacky enough to pick up a light item but not so tacky that it will not drop an item into position.

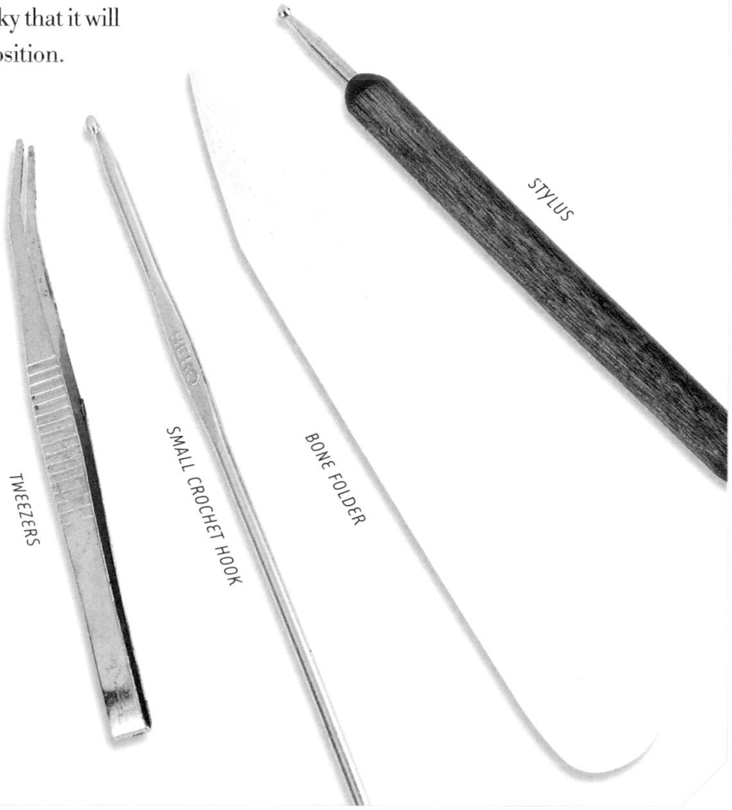

STYLUS

TWEEZERS

SMALL CROCHET HOOK

BONE FOLDER

TAPES and ADHESIVES

You will find that, as an artist, you may very well have a use for every single tape on the market, but let's stick to the tapes used in this book. Keep in mind that this book centers on quick gifts and not necessarily archival gifts. Most common tapes will dry out over time and should not be considered archival unless identified as such on the packaging.

The projects in this book use the following tapes:

- *Sticky backed foil tape* from USArtQuest, available in brass, copper and silver. It sticks to just about anything and can be aged with liver-of-sulfur or Silver/Black.
- *Self-adhesive, brown paper-shipping tape.* I love this stuff for making quick little books.
- *Masking tape*
- *Black masking tape*
- *Double-stick foam tape*
- *Double-stick masking tape*

You can find most of these tapes at stamp stores, office supply stores and/or hardware stores.

Another item that you will use plenty of is glue. As with just about every art tool, there are no right or wrongs here—just good and better choices. Use the best glue for the product that you are working with and you will be much happier with the finished project.

For speed

For fast results when gluing paper-to-paper, I recommend a **QUICK-DRYING LIQUID ADHESIVE**. My favorite is a little rolling applicator of glue by Pentel called Roll 'N Glue. It grabs fast, lays flat and dries quickly.

For leather

LEATHERCRAFT CEMENT has become a favorite, not only for leathercraft, but for bookbinding with paper and cover boards as well. It is extremely strong when used as contact cement. Coat both sides completely and let dry. This will only take about five minutes. Press both pieces together, hold for about ten seconds and it will be set. You can find this product at The Leather Factory.

For fabric

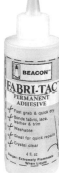

My all-time favorite product is the **FABRI-TAC PERMANENT ADHESIVE** from Beacon Adhesives Company. This product grabs fast and dries fast. It contains acetone, so follow the directions provided on the labels and work safely.

DRITZ FRAY CHECK works beautifully to stop fraying. Run a thin line of glue along the edges on ribbon and fabric and let dry. A dab of Fray Check on knots will keep them from coming undone.

Other options

A **GLUE GUN AND GLUE STICKS** are a fast way to glue, obviously, but they can also be used to make stamped pendants or to apply dimensional foiling to projects.

PADDING COMPOUND, which you can get from paper stores, is for making the perfect binding on notebooks.

POSTER TACK is actually quite strong when stuck to a nonporous surface like metal. You can use it in place of foam tape, and it is especially useful for odd shapes.

DIAMOND GLAZE works as a shiny top coat, but it does double duty as a glue for holding charms, beads, Roxs and fibers to your work. It is not a quick-grab glue, so, in the interest of making quick gifts, you may want to use one of the other adhesives listed above.

TRADITIONAL SUPPLIES

◎ Leathers

Leather is easy to use and easy to stamp on. Just about any stamp artist already has a variety of coloring materials to use on leather. (You can seal watercolors with a spray sealant.) Leather works great for book covers, pins, barrettes ... the list goes on.

Almost Leather from Comotion is a fun alternative to real hide. A foam rubber type of product, Almost Leather may be heated and stamped for a tooled look.

◎ Other media

TIN SHEETS are useful for making jewelry, assemblage and other ornaments. I get mine from cookie tins at thrift stores. You can usually find large tins for about fifty cents each. If they are not out on the shelves, ask the clerk about them. Thrift stores often keep the holiday tins in the storeroom until they are in season. Remember to use your gloves when you cut the sheets with tin snips. Use a metal file to smooth the cut edges.

WIRE MESH of any type adds texture and dimension to your work. The open weave is suited to further embellishment with beads and fibers. Look in art and craft stores as well as hardware stores.

SEQUIN WASTE is what is left over after the factories cut the sequins from the shiny plastic ribbon. You can find spools of it in floral, craft and some fabric stores. Also look for it in the discount or surplus fabric stores.

WOODEN BEADS, hearts and other shapes are found in craft stores and in some fabric stores. These wood pieces take ink very well, can be colored with most materials and are useful for a number of projects.

MATERIALS ON HAND

You may already have most of these supplies on hand, but if you don't, they are easy to find at just about any stamp, craft or fabric store.

- *gold and copper wire* (20-gauge)
- *copper wire* in several gauges
- *tin fleur de lis* from Loose Ends
- *pretty fibers and cords* from knitting stores
- *⅝" (2cm) grosgrain ribbon* from fabric stores
- *brown linen beading thread* from bead stores
- *glass marbles* (with a flat end)
- *thumbtacks* (get the flat-head type)
- *gold plastic leaf* to add to your gifts
- *plain barrettes* from fabric or craft stores
- *silver bracelet* from bead stores
- *glass beads* from bead, craft or fabric stores
- *tassels* from craft or fabric stores
- *rusted leaves* from craft stores
- *vanilla potpourri*
- *cotton balls*
- *butterfly hair clip* from discount stores or beauty supply stores

FAVORITE CUTTERS

TIN SNIPS

- *paper edgers*
- *corner edgers*
- *rotary cutter*
- *craft knife*
- *utility knife*
- *leather scissors* (Possibly an extravagant item, but if you cut a lot of leather they are worth the price.)
- *tin snips*
- *decorative scissors*
- *three pairs of straight scissors* (Mark a separate pair of craft scissors for paper, fabric and metal/plastic and use them accordingly.)
- *leather hole punch*
- *eyelet setter and eyelets*
- *paper hole punch*

ROTARY CUTTER

UTILITY KNIFE

LEATHER HOLE PUNCH

LEATHER SCISSORS

DECORATIVE SCISSORS

EYELET SETTER

EYELETS

READY, SET, GO!

The secret to making quick gifts is to keep it simple and work in neutral colors or color combinations you know and like. You can easily spend a couple of hours on color choice alone. If you make something in colors you're not happy with, you'll get frustrated trying to fix the mistake. So, for speed, keep your colors familiar and safe. Here are specific tips to keep your craft project under thirty minutes.

◎ Tip One

When you can, go for a rustic, earthy look. That means you can leave raw edges and take advantage of the natural colors of the materials you are using. Chipboard and corrugated cardboard are good materials to leave as is.

◎ Tip Two

Cut out the time-consuming details. For instance, use a clear-drying glue to glue beads on instead of sewing them on. I know this will drive my purist beading friends crazy, but look at the Leather Band project on pages 88-91. Surrounding the larger beads with tiny glass beads looks great and gives no hint that you skimped on time.

◎ Tip Three

Use inexpensive purchased materials when you can. For instance, use ready-made papier mâché boxes; don't make them from scratch as in my first book. Use rusted metal and wood shapes available in craft stores. Scour the sales bins to look for base

project materials. I just bought some Christmas cookie tins at an after-Christmas sale for 90% off. A bargain anyway, but when you hold the tin over an open flame (like a gas stove), the painted holiday images will burn off. This gives you some aged-looking and useful tin to use as is or to cut up and use in projects such as the desk shrine (see pages 65-68). Most dollar stores even have tin snips that work just fine for this book's projects.

SAFETY PRECAUTION: *When you are burning off paint or working with any product with fumes, wear a painter's mask, open the windows and turn on the fans. If possible, work out-of-doors.*

◎ Tip Four

For clocks, go to the dollar stores and buy those poor ugly duckling clocks. After tearing them apart, you'll have perfectly good battery-operated clockworks.

◎ Tip Five

Keep a collection of small charms, beads, buttons and even smashed bottle caps that you find on the roadside. Any little thing like small game pieces, broken Tinkertoys, rusted metal washers, metal screen, fancy fibers and junk jewelry are fair game for assemblage.

◎ Tip Six

Save the scraps of stamped and colored papers that are left over from previous projects. A lot of my hurried projects, cards and class samples are made from previously stamped and colored papers from the scrap box.

◎ Tip Seven

To acquire fancy fibers at an awesome price, go to thrift shops and buy sweaters made from interesting yarns. Take a snip and start unraveling. This will give you plenty of scrap yarn to work with. Add to that metallic and cotton crochet thread and you will have very fancy fibers indeed. Also, look for old tablecloths, curtains and bedspreads. They often have loose weaves with excellent fibers.

◎ Tip Eight

You can get some neat wings for things by taking big butterfly hair clips and cutting off the wings. If they are metallic, burn those too. All the paint and glitter will burn off, leaving excellent rustic-looking tin. Remember to wear your mask and work in an area with good ventilation.

◎ Tip Nine

For speed in your work, itemize materials and keep them in separate baggies and little boxes in a drawer. That way you will be able to lay your hands on exactly what item, shape or texture you need when you are in a hurry.

◎ Tip Ten

Finally, remember to look at everything with fresh eyes and always with your art in mind.

1 Art-a-TACS

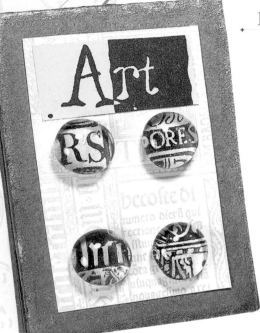

PLAIN THUMBTACKS get a jolt of energy from your graphic artwork. A person can always use tacks, and these heart-grabbers look stunning when used on tiebacks, books, boxes or furniture. OK, OK– they're great for bulletin boards too!

As a time-saver, I left the corrugated edges of the cardboard exposed for a utilitarian look. You can certainly cover them with tape or paper if you prefer.

Materials

- four flat-head tacks
- four flat-end glass marbles
- two pieces of corrugated cardboard cut to 2½" x 3" (6cm x 8cm)
- stamps (I used ones from Stampers Anonymous)
- black and straw-colored inkpads
- Color Dusters

- colored pencils
- clear, quick-drying glue
- Crafter's Pick The Ultimate glue (a clear-drying white glue)
- cream cardstock
- scissors
- utility knife

OPTIONAL
- double-sided tape

1] Stamp your first packaging image on cream cardstock and set aside.

2] Stamp your second packaging image and set aside.

3] Stamp in black ink the images that will appear under the marbles. Add detail with Color Dusters and colored pencils.

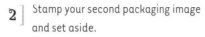

5] Use a clear, quick-drying glue to attach the image to the glass marble.

4] Cut the image pieces that will fit under the marbles. Remember to cut them a little smaller than the marble so the paper edges do not stick out past the marble's edge.

6] Glue the marble to the tack with Crafter's Pick The Ultimate glue.

7] To make a thick thumbtack holder, use a utility knife to cut two pieces of corrugated cardboard the same size.

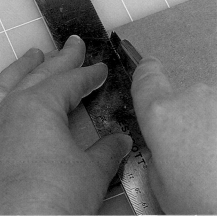

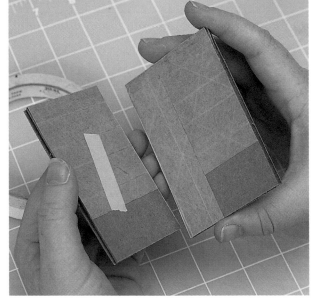

8] A piece of double-sided tape will hold the two pieces of cardboard together nicely. Put double-sided tape on the cardboard and remove the paper backing to expose the tape's sticky part. Firmly press the two pieces of cardboard together.

9] Cut out the packaging images. Glue them onto the cardboard.

2 Beautiful BOOKENDS

HOW ABOUT DRESSING UP some plain bookends? The usefulness of a bookend, and especially a bookend that has been gilded by you, makes a great gift for all occasions.

Of course, the beads and the Amazing Glaze are an optional touch, as is the gold gilding pen. If you are short on time, think about skipping some of these steps. Your bookend will still be fabulous!

Materials

- metal bookends
- stamps (the swirl stamp is from Hero Arts and the checked stamp is from Magenta Rubber Stamps)
- thin chipboard
- gold Krylon gilding pen
- clear embossing ink
- gold and green embossing powder
- Amazing Glaze embossing powder
- wire mesh
- glue gun
- heat gun
- scissors

OPTIONAL
- little beads
- gold plastic leaf

1│ Use the metal bookend as a template. Trace the outline onto the chipboard and cut it out. Cut a little smaller than the traced image.

2│ Stamp and emboss the swirl design onto the chipboard.

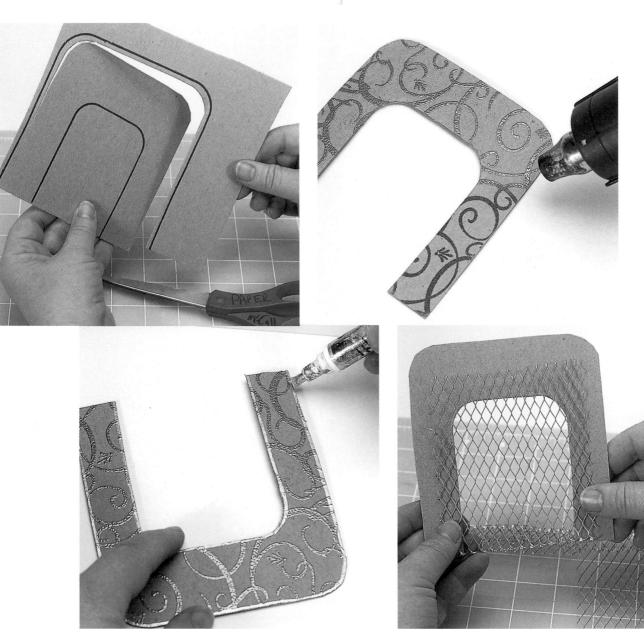

3│ Run the gilding pen along the edges of the chipboard to outline it.

4│ Cut the wire mesh a little smaller than the outside edge of the chipboard frame. Remember not to use your good scissors to cut the metal or the chipboard.

5] Use the glue gun to fix the mesh to the bookend.

6] Glue the chipboard frame over the wire. Work fast so the glue stays soft long enough for you to press it flat.

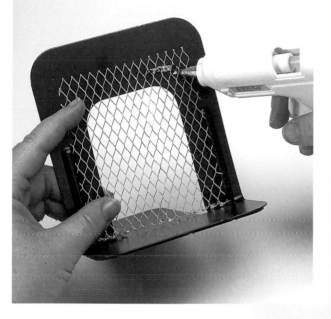

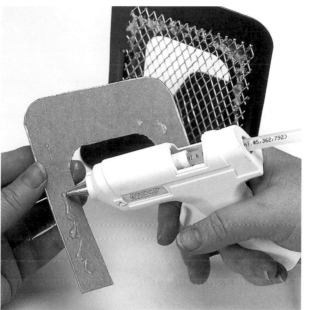

7] Stamp a little embellishment and emboss with green powder.

8] **Optional Step:** Use the gilding pen to add a bit of detail to the chipboard charm.

tip

If the **hot glue hardens** before you can position the frame or if you need to reposition it, use the heat gun to quickly remelt the glue.

9 ⌉ Tap clear embossing ink all over the embellishment and then emboss with Amazing Glaze. While the first coat is still hot, sprinkle more powder and reheat. Repeat this step three times.

10 ⌉ **Optional Step:** Drop little beads into the glaze while it is still hot and liquid. You can use the heat gun to melt the glaze a little more to secure the beads. You may want to add another coat on top of the beads if they do not seem secure enough.

11 ⌉ Hot glue the embellishments to the front of the bookend.

3 ⟳ small BOOK

CREATE dozens of delightful announcements, party favors, wedding keepsakes—you name it. Small books make great gifts and this one is no exception. The idea for this little cutie came from a secondhand find of several rolls of calculator tape. It is perfect for quick little accordion-fold books because you do not have to measure and cut the long lengths of paper.

Materials

- calculator tape
- chipboard for the covers
- bone folder or stylus
- stamp and dye ink (I used products from JudiKins, Stamp Oasis and Clearsnap)
- quick-drying glue
- embossing ink and powder

- double-sided foam tape
- ⅝" (2cm) grosgrain ribbon
- utility knife
- cutting mat
- straightedge
- scissors

1] With a utility knife, cut the chipboard pieces so they will be $1/4$" (6mm) larger than the width of the calculator tape and as long as you want your covers to be. In this case, my covers are cut to 2" x $2 1/4$" (5cm x 6cm). Stamp them. For speed, I used the exposed chipboard with a simple stamp. You could certainly cover the chipboard for a more elegant look.

2] An easy way to mark your fold lines for this project is to line up the paper on the grid of a cutting mat and score it every 2" (5cm). This tape is narrow enough that I can just run the bone folder along the printed grid line. If you want to be more precise, use a straight-edge and run the bone folder along it for a crisp line.

3] Follow the scored lines to fold the text block into a nice accordion packet.

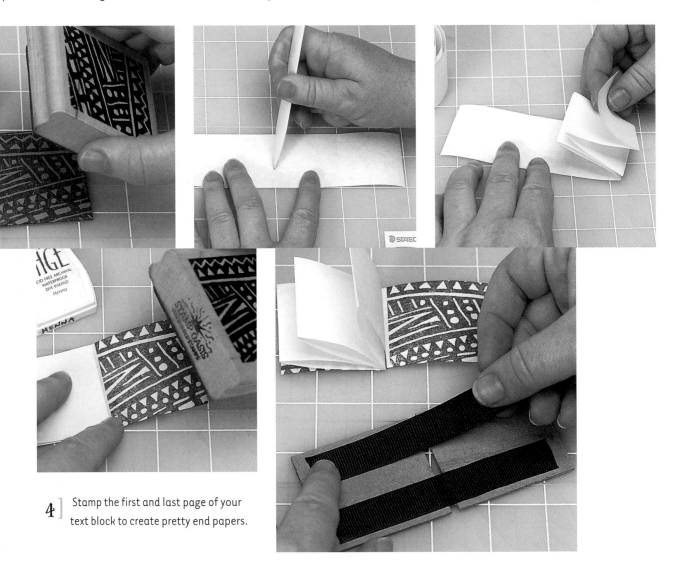

4] Stamp the first and last page of your text block to create pretty end papers.

5] Lay the covers about $1/8$" (3mm) apart and glue the ribbons across them. The width of the spine space is determined by how wide your text block is going to be. A text block of several folded pages will require a wider space for the spine.

6] Glue the end papers onto the chipboard covers, leaving the inside edge of the text block free of glue.

7] Stamp and emboss a center medallion.

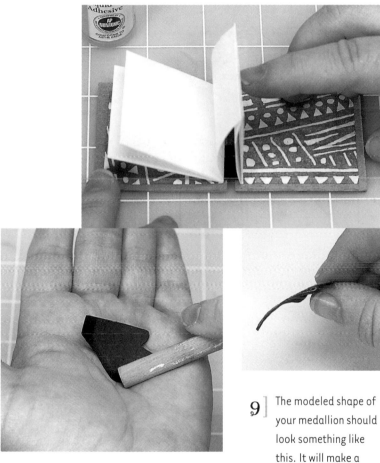

8] Cup the medallion in your palm and run a pen across the edges to model them.

9] The modeled shape of your medallion should look something like this. It will make a nicer finish to your project because the medallion's edge will drape over and hide the foam tape.

10] Attach the double-sided foam tape to the medallion, and adhere it to the front cover of the book.

Colorful Jewelry HOLDER

HERE IS NUMBER FIVE on the list of ten
thousand things to do with these bookends. They make
great shrines! Speaking of shrines, what better way
to provide a colorful home for your most cherished
jewels? I used sequin waste to create a funky look
on this project, but wire mesh makes for a
stronger support. You could also spray
paint the plastic grid material that is used
for needlepoint with thicker yarns. If you
have a whole day to play and experiment,
you might want to think about stamping
clay to embellish the stand.

Materials

- metal bookends
- Almost Leather
  (from Comotion)
- stamps (the guys are from
  Comotion and the unmounted
  stamps are from Claudia Rose)
- black Crafter's ink
- black fine-point Sharpie marker
- heat gun
- sponge and sponge brush
- small metal container

- metallic paints for metal
  surfaces (I used Luna Lights
  from Stamp Oasis)
- sequin waste (purchased at
  floral supply stores and some
  craft stores)
- Fabri-Tac glue or glue gun
- scissors

OPTIONAL
- thin chipboard or posterboard
- gel pens

1 | Ink your stamp with the Crafter's ink and set it aside. Heat the Almost Leather until it takes on a light shine. It will curl a little, but don't worry about that.

2 | Stamp firmly into the hot "leather" and hold it for a second. (The heat will help set the Crafter's ink.) If you did not get a good impression, you can turn the Almost Leather over, reheat and restamp.

3 | Cut out the image, leaving a border. Put a couple of colors of Luna Lights onto a plate and use your fingers to dab color onto the stamped image.

4 | Use a permanent marker to touch up the lines, if necessary.

5 | **Optional Step:** Use gel pens to add more detail if you like.

6 | With a sponge brush, add paint to the stamps. Randomly stamp all over the bookend.

7 | Use the tip of the paint-laden sponge brush to add more texture.

8 | Cut the sequin waste to fit inside the raised edges on the stand. Use Fabri-Tac, a glue gun or some other quick-drying glue to set it in place on the backside of the bookend.

9 | Use the Fabri-Tac to glue the stamped image onto the front of the bookend.

10 **Optional Step:** Trace and cut out a thin piece of chipboard and paint it black, or cut a black piece of posterboard and glue it to the back of your bookend.

11 Sponge the Luna Lights onto a little metal container. These containers are called watchmaker's parts cases.

12 Be careful not to get any paint on the inside of the lid or the top outer rim of the container. This will keep the lid and the body from sticking together when closed.

13 Use the Fabri-Tac to glue the container to the front of the jewelry shrine.

Additional project idea

You could glue a larger container to the back of the stand for more storage. Think of how cute this stand would look if you glued an inexpensive plastic pencil holder to the back and made the stamped image out of a thick corkboard, backed with chipboard for stability. Then you could use the little cups for paper clips and enclose your Art-a-Tacs (see page 20) as part of the gift.

Fabric Notebook COVER

FOR A QUICK START to fabric projects, choose a pretty, muted fabric pattern that will allow your stamped work to show on top. By varying the size, this same project can easily be adapted to make a cover for a makeup brush set, a cover to house a watercolor pad with brushes, or a paint pallet with pencils and pens. A little imagination yields a very thoughtful gift.

In the interest of teaching you as much as possible in one book, I have also included directions for making your own notepads. A purchased pad will work just as well if you're short on time.

Materials

- fabric for the front and back of the notebook
- pen and notepad
- stamps (I used ones from JudiKins and Hero Arts)
- fusible webbing and stiff fusible interfacing
- iron

- Fabri-Tac glue
- FolkArt metallic paints
- Apple Barrel matte acrylic paints
- sponge brush
- 18" (46cm) braid, about half a yard
- button, needle-nose pliers and piece of wire for the closure

- cutting mat
- straightedge
- rotary cutter
- scissors

OPTIONAL
- JudiKins solvent-based cleaner

1   Cut two pieces of fabric—one for the front cover and one for the back cover; one piece of stiff, fusible interfacing; and one piece of fusible webbing. Assemble them as shown, with the right sides of the fabric facing outward. The fusible interfacing has the fusing material on only one side. You'll need the extra webbing to fuse the layers together. Iron flat.

2   After the fabric packet has cooled, line it up on the grid of the cutting mat and trim to the size and shape you prefer, using a rotary cutter and straightedge. Cut the fabric so the folder extends 1' (1m) over the top and bottom of the notepad. It should be twice the width of the pad, plus allow about 1" (3cm) for the pen and about 2" (5cm) for the front flap.

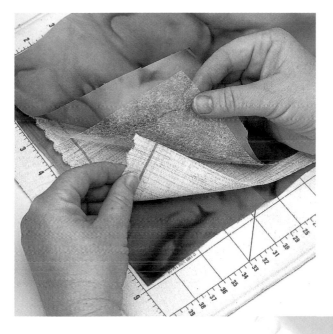

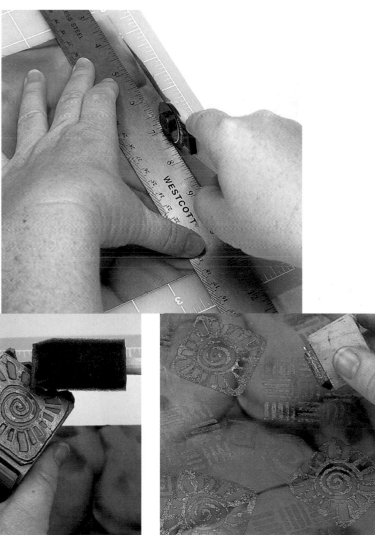

3   Use a sponge brush to dab acrylic paint onto a stamp. A light matte color, like yellow or white acrylic paint, will add opacity to the metallic paint.

4   Stamp randomly over the fabric in a variety of colors.

5 | Water will get wet acrylic paint off your stamps, but if you don't want to wash them until you are done stamping, JudiKins solvent-based cleaner will remove dried acrylic paint from rubber. Put the cleaner directly onto the stamp, wait a couple of seconds, and then use a terry cloth rag to wipe the paint and cleaner away.

6 | Put glue along the edge of the cover. Position the braid so that it will fold over to cover the raw edges of the fabric. Glue it down on one side, then flip it over and glue the braid down on the other side.

8 | For easy sizing of the pen holder, snugly wrap the pen with a piece of braid and glue one end over the other. Be careful not to glue the pen to the braid.

9 | Put a dab of fabric glue on the over-lapped braid and hold the pen assembly in place until the glue sets.

7 | Cut a piece of braid a little wider than the notepad. Slide the braid under a few of the last pages for positioning. Fold the ends of the braid under and glue into position.

tip

Fabric glue dries quickly,
but for extra speed, a
glue gun can be used
in place of the Fabri-Tac.

10   Curl the ends of a piece of wire with pliers, and then stick it through a button and the fabric.

[**Optional**]

Sometimes you will find a fabric with a simple design that can be easily translated into a carved stamp. This book cover has been stamped and embossed in gold powder. You can emboss on fabric, but be sure not to over-cook the powder or it will melt right into the fabric and disappear.

11   Tie one end of the cord around the button. The closure is a simple wrap. (For instructions on a shrink-plastic button, see pages 38–40.)

A SET OF THESE buttons would make a great gift all by themselves. Any of your friends who craft will welcome the time and effort that you put into these shrink-plastic buttons, which they can add to their own art.

Of course, these buttons also make a wonderful addition to your own art. I have used black shrink plastic for this project, but the clear, ivory, white and brown shrink plastic work just as well. If you do not have black shrink plastic, color the clear plastic with a black Sharpie and proceed as usual.

Materials

+ black shrink plastic
+ heat gun
+ scissors
+ FolkArt metallic paints
+ gold or silver Krylon gilding pen
+ ¼"(6mm) hole punch or a drill
+ stamp (I used one from Hero Arts)
+ Treasure Crystal Cote
+ black Sharpie marker
+ disposable brush

1 Cut the plastic into any shape you like. A bold design cut with decorative scissors gives a nice edging to the buttons.

2 Use a ¼" (6mm) hole punch to make buttonholes.

3 Heat the plastic until it stops shrinking. Remember: Do not heat items on your cutting mat. (The photo below is an example of do as I say, not as I did.)

4 Jam a stamp into the hot plastic and hold for a couple of seconds. The plastic will pop right off the stamp when it cools down. If your impression is not deep enough, reheat the plastic until the design disappears and restamp.

5 Although you have prepunched the holes, they will sometimes close up after you stamp into the plastic. You can use a pin vise with a drill bit to redrill the holes.

Important Note
I used the heat gun this close for illustration purposes only. A Milwaukee gun is very hot and will cause the plastic to curl and stick to itself if you hold it too close. Keep about 5" (13cm) away from the plastic to start. Have patience. A low heat will produce a more controlled shrink. Getting the gun this close should only happen after the shrinking has stopped and you move in closer for a final heating to make the plastic soft. The plastic will curl toward the heat source, so keep that in mind when pointing the gun.

6 The top colors will show up a lot better if you put a basecoat of silver or gold gilding pen on the black plastic.

7 Use your fingers to dab small and variegated amounts of the metallic paint onto the raised portion of the button.

9] Nothing gives a high-gloss coat like Treasure Crystal Cote. I don't even clean my brush after the last use. I just let it dry hard. When I dip it into the bottle the next time, I can swirl the Treasure Crystal Cote around in the cap and the solvent will soften the brush again.

8] If you get color down into the design, you can use a black Sharpie to cover it up.

10] Paint the entire button with a coat of glaze and let dry.

hint

When you have a lot of buttons or other small objects to color and coat, lay a strip of **double-sided tape** on a scrap mat or chipboard. Place the buttons on the tape and then color and coat them. This is particularly useful for spray painting small objects.

Quick NOTEPADS

PADDING YOUR OWN BOOKS is quick, easy and inexpensive. It also allows you to use any paper in any size that you like. A long time ago, banks used to pad new one-dollar bills together so you could give them as gifts. I still think it makes a great gift for children. They like paying for their own purchases, and tearing a dollar off of a special pad makes them feel even more important. A simple stamped piece of cardstock, scored and glued to the padded spine, makes a nice cover for the money book.

Materials

- stack of cut paper
- padding compound
- paintbrush
- weight, such as a brick or heavy stack of books
- paper tape to cover the padded edge or a piece of cardstock to wrap it like a little paperback book
- cutting mat

1 | You can get a ream of paper cut to any size that you like from almost any paper store or printing house. They usually charge per cut, so be prepared to pay that way. A ream of paper that is cut into three stacks would count as two cuts if they put the whole ream into the cutter at one time. Some print houses will claim that a cut can only be done on one hundred sheets at a time, so a ream of five hundred sheets would be five cuts instead of one.

There is a huge self-help copy house in the United States, which shall remain nameless, that has many branches across the country and they all vary in practice. Call around for prices to get the best deal and to avoid the aggravation of a clerk who claims the machine will cut only one hundred sheets at a time.

2 | I pad as many papers as I can at one time, or as many as I can easily hold in my hands. Then I always have a pad on hand when I need it. Tamp the stack of papers together. Lining them up on the grid of your cutting mat will help you align the paper. Place a weight as close to the edge as possible.

3 Padding compound can be found at almost any print shop or paper company. I get mine at Kelly Paper. I am still working on my first jar. I bought the huge pink jar of compound because it was on sale for a great price. I poured a little into a baby food jar so I could easily ship it for photography purposes. The pink works great, but it will show if you accidentally smear some on the edge of the pad, so buy the white compound if you can. Use the brush to paint the compound onto the spine edge of the stack of papers. Don't worry if it gets on the plastic mat. When the compound dries, it will peel right off.

4 You can put a cover sheet over the first page of the pad to protect it if you want. When I use an inexpensive paper such as white bond, I just tear off the top sheet that may have been marred by the weight (brick) used in step 2.

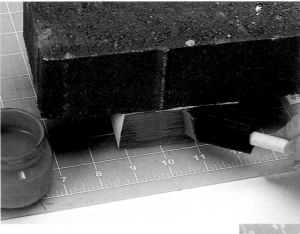

5 Tear the pad apart for the size that you need to use.

6 Use a piece of paper tape to secure the edge of the pad.

Stamp and Stationery SET

TAKE A carving block or cutting material and cut, scratch or gouge your way to a wonderful stamp and stationery set for a special and totally unique gift. Use forks, screwdrivers, awls—whatever will make a mark in a clever way. No eraser carving could be easier than this.

Materials

- carving block
  (I used one from Staedtler. It is smooth on all sides so that you can even carve borders on the stamp edges if you like.)
- forks, awls, screwdrivers
  (the Phillips head makes a cute little star pattern)—anything that will make a mark in the eraser

- matte cardstock
- dye inkpad
- scissors
- quick-drying glue

1] Make your marks into the carving block. Check the image by stamping it onto cardstock and add more details if necessary.

2] Stamp directly onto good cardstock in a pleasing design.

3] If you find that you have mis-stamped and you no longer like the design on the card, do not fret. Continue to cover the entire piece of paper.

4] Cut the stamped paper into long, slightly diagonal strips.

5] Use quick-drying glue to position the strips onto a new backing card.

Final Touch
Tie up the stationery packet and give the carved stamp, some extra blank cards and a little stamp pad as part of the gift.

9 Inspirational BOOKMARK

A PRETTY BOOKMARK is made all the more outstanding with the addition of an inspirational saying like the one on this stamp from Hero Arts. The preprinted fabric and the ease of making multiple bookmarks make these excellent gifts for a large group of friends. I used fabric for this project but a heavyweight, handmade paper would make an elegant bookmark as well.

Take Time to Enjoy The Simple Things in Life

Materials

- fabric with a light, muted design suitable for stamping
- fusible interfacing
- iron
- stamps (I used ones from Hero Arts)
- black Crafter's ink
- FolkArt metallic paint
- foam brush
- metallic and glitter gel pens
- ¼" (6mm) brass eyelet and an eyelet setter

- tassel (I used one from JudiKins)
- scissors or rotary cutter
- straightedge
- cutting mat

OPTIONAL

- acrylic paints and a stamp you carved yourself
- fabric glue and ribbon

1] Place the fabric face side down onto the ironing board, lay the fusible interfacing on top of that, and then place the fabric face side up to complete the stack.

2] Fuse the fabric together with an iron per the webbing instructions.

3] I made two bookmarks here to show you how to make multiple bookmarks. I cut them apart after they are completely colored with stamping and pen work. Stamp your inspirational saying in black Crafter's ink.

4] Stamp the flowers with the Crafter's ink and then set the whole piece with an iron.

5] **Optional Step:** Put metallic paint on your foam brush and use it as an inkpad. Be sure to ink the stamp evenly and with a nice, light coat of paint. (Do not worry if the acrylic paint dries onto your stamp. The JudiKins stamp cleaner will clean it right off the rubber.)

6] Stamp a variety of designs and colors along the edges and down the middle of the bookmarks, keeping in mind where you will cut them apart.

7] **Optional Step:** Use gel pens for added detail and cut the bookmarks apart when you're happy with your stamp work. For ease in cutting, use a cutting mat, straightedge and rotary cutter. I don't even measure the bookmarks; I just follow the grid lines on the cutting mat with my rotary cutter.

8] Cut a little X where the eyelet will go. Be sure to not make it too large.

9] Place the eyelet onto the setter as shown.

10] Place the eyelet into the X and crimp it with the setter.

11] Tie the tassel onto the eyelet.

[Optional Embellishments]

You can paint the edge of the bookmark with acrylic paints. This will keep the edges from fraying. You can also use a permanent black ink pen for detail work and a stamp that you carved yourself for the design.

Another optional edging:

Use fabric glue to attach a pretty cord or ribbon around the perimeter of the bookmark.

10 ❖ Pyramid CLOCK

INEXPENSIVE CLOCKS can be found everywhere these days. The clock in this project came from a dollar store. You can't beat that price for a clock finding! These inexpensive clocks are easy to take apart. Even if the hands are too long, simply take your craft scissors and cut the hands to the shape and size that you like. Want a different color? Paint them!

Although this chipboard base is easy and inexpensive to construct, there are tons of other base ideas that are just as easy to make. Consider, for instance, making a clock with the simple bent metal shape from the Simple Shrine project on pages 65-68.

Materials

- ✦ clockworks
- ✦ piece of sturdy chipboard
- ✦ pyramid template (see page 120)
- ✦ stamps and inkpads [I used stamps from JudiKins and Zettiology Rubber Stamps & Mythos (Teesha Moore); the pigment and dye inks are from Clearsnap]
- ✦ tape
- ✦ stylus or bone folder
- ✦ awl
- ✦ a cork or piece of foamcore board
- ✦ utility knife
- ✦ cutting mat
- ✦ straightedge
- ✦ scissors
- ✦ black marker

OPTIONAL
- ✦ cream cardstock
- ✦ quick-drying glue
- ✦ jewelry findings

1] Cut a pattern of the pyramid and transfer it to your chipboard.

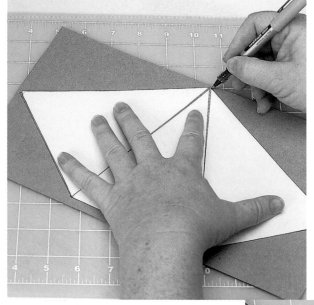

2] Use a utility knife and a straightedge to cut out the pyramid shape.

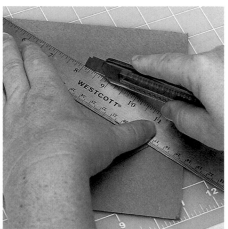

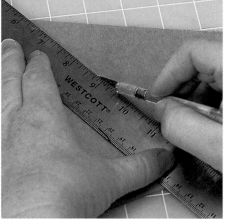

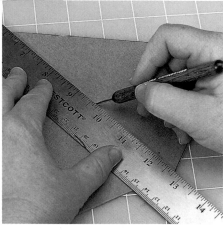

3] Score along the fold lines with the knife, then flip the piece over and score the fold lines with a stylus or bone folder.

4] Fold the pyramid so that the knife score is on the outside fold line.

5] Shape the pyramid. Make sure the sides meet and are the same length and that it will sit properly. Trim the ends if necessary.

6] Stamp the chipboard with a multicolored design.

7] Stamp the letters in black dye ink.

8 ⎤ Center the tape as shown.

9 ⎤ Join the edges and fold the tape over and down, pressing firmly to secure it.

10 ⎤ Use a touch-up pen on your stamping if necessary.

11 ⎤ Disassemble the clock, noting the order of the hands. They are usually lined up with the hour hand closest to the clock face, the minute hand next and the second hand on top.

12] Put a little bit of ink on the nib and mark the chipboard with it.

13] Resting the clock on a cork or piece of foamcore board, use the awl to make a hole in the chipboard.

14] You may need to work the awl around and use a knife to widen the hole so that the clockworks can fit into it.

15 Fit the clockworks into place.

16 Place the clock hands onto the workings.

17 Make sure that the hands will clear the bottom of the clock when they turn. You may need to trim the hands with craft scissors to fit.

18 Use a black marker to trim the bottom edge of the clock.

[Optional Embellishments]

Cut out and glue the stamped image into place with quick-drying glue.

Stamp an image onto cream cardstock.

Glue on jewelry findings for additional trim.

11 ⊙ Runner WONDER

A WONDER OF A BOOKLET

made from—believe it or not—a floor runner!

You can even heat the material and stamp it for a

cool intaglio effect. This booklet is a great size

for your purse, and the runner cover makes it

virtually indestructible.

Materials

- floor runner
- paper for the text block
- bone folder or stylus
- length of string, piece of wire and button
- awl and a cork or piece of foamcore board
- needle-nose pliers
- brick or weight
- utility knife

- cutting mat
- straightedge
- scissors

OPTIONAL

- stamp and gold metallic pigment ink
  (the stamps are from Stamp Oasis; the ink is from Clearsnap)
- quick-drying glue
- heat gun

1 | Cut the runner to size. This one is cut to 4⅝" x 7" (11cm x 18cm). Use a straightedge and utility knife to score the runner and fold along the center spine.

2 | Crease the spine.

3 | Set a brick or weight on the cover to set the shape.

4 | Cut and fold together as many pieces of paper as you want for the text block.

5] Pay attention to the splayed edges. If they splay out too far, you can split the pages into several signatures and sew them into the book individually.

6] To trim the text block edges, lay down a straightedge and put pressure on it. While holding it secure, use a utility knife with a new blade and cut straight down.

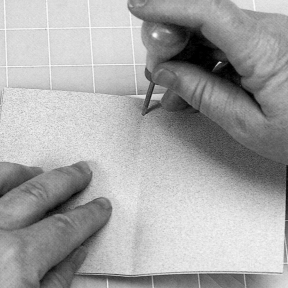

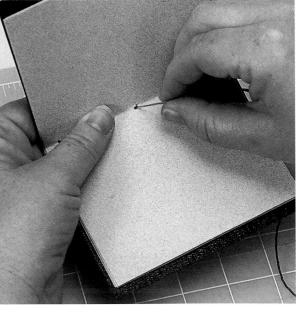

7] To make a simple pamphlet stitch, punch three holes into the spine of the text block. Place a hole at each end of the book, about ½" (1cm) from the edge and then place a hole in the center. Transfer the holes to the cover.

8] Sew into the center hole.

9] Bring the thread across to the end and sew up into the inside spine.

10] Span the length of the spine with the thread and sew out of the last hole.

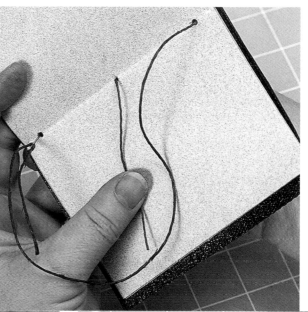

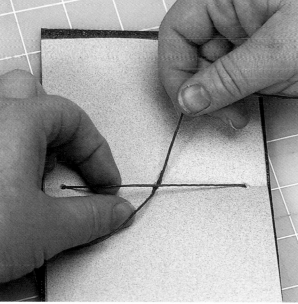

11] Sew back up into the spine through the center hole. Let the ends of the thread fall on either side of the long center thread and tie a square knot over it.

12] Clip the ends of the string, leaving a ½" (1cm) tail.

13 Lay the cover over a cork or piece of foamcore board and punch two holes in the cover for the button closure.

14 Form a piece of wire into a staple shape over a button. Slide the wire through the button and into the punched holes of the cover.

15 Use the needle-nose pliers to flatten the wire and twirl it into a shape that will hold the button in place.

16 Tie a length of cord around the button.

17 Bring the cord around and loop it over the button for a closure.

[**Optional** Embellishments]

Ink a stamp with pigment ink. Heat a square of floor runner until it starts to look shiny and curls up at the edges.

While the rubber is still hot and soft, stamp firmly and hold a few seconds.

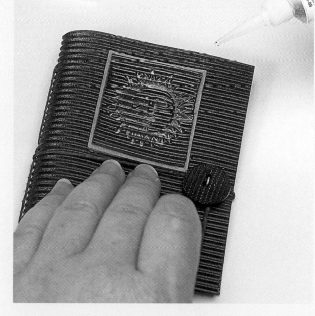

Use a quick-drying glue to fix the medallion into place. I have glued it on a piece of chipboard in this instance. Note: Glue from a glue gun will not hold onto this rubber.

12 ❂ Shade PULL

THIS SIMPLE PROJECT works equally well as an avant-garde shade pull, lamp pull, drapery tieback, book medallion—even a necklace! So many options and so little expenditure. This is a very quick, very cool gift if ever there was one.

Materials

- rectangular piece of wood
- stamp
  (I used one from Postmodern Design)
- coal Ancient Page permanent ink
- Staedtler red brush marker
- gold Krylon gilding pen
- pin vise or drill
- black cording
- gold 20-gauge wire
- several beads in various sizes
- three 3" (7.6cm) head pins
- pencil or ¼" (6mm) dowel
- needle-nose pliers

1] Ink the portion of the stamp that you want on your pull with black permanent ink. For more accurate positioning, bring the wood to the stamp and press firmly.

2] Color the edges with a permanent marker.

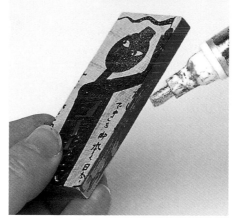

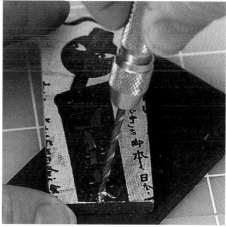

3] Drybrush the edges of the pull with a gold pen.

4] Drill a hole at the top for the cord and holes at the bottom for the dangles.

5] Make the dangles by threading the beads onto a head pin and making a connection loop. Create smaller sections by making eye pins out of the wire, threading a bead or two onto the wire and looping the parts together. Use large jump rings to connect the dangles to the wood.

6] Use the needle-nose pliers to close the jump rings.

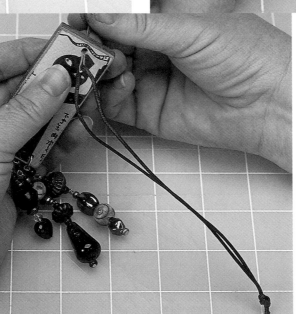

8] Slip the cord ends into the loop and pull up. Tie the ends of the cord together with a simple overhand knot.

7] For the top cord, fold a length of thin cord in half and slip the folded section into the drilled hole to make a loop.

13 ❖ simple SHRINE

SOMETIMES you just want a simple little sculpture at which to gaze. Capturing ages of Italian drama, this shrine takes you on a journey of artful fantasy. You can make your shrine as a sculpture for your desk or as something more functional. This simple shape can also be a base for a clock or a larger assemblage.

Materials

- scrap piece of burned tin
- stamp
  (I used one from Stampers Anonymous)
- tin fleur-de-lis (from a garland purchased from Loose Ends)
- JudiKins black permanent ink for nonporous surfaces
- felt pad
- poster tack
  (get the orange, not the blue; stuff-it sticks to tin better)
- tin snips and gloves
- metal file
- needle-nose pliers
- plastic plate or cardstock wrapped in foil

OPTIONAL

- awl or nail and hammer for punching holes

1] It's important to wear your work gloves when you cut this tin. It can bite hard. For this project, I cut up a big tin can that originally held popcorn. You can get these cans inexpensively at just about any thrift store. If they are not in season (most of them have Christmas designs on them), ask the store manager about them. They usually have a stockpile waiting for the holidays to roll around.

2] Wear your mask when you burn paint off tin. It is a lacquer-based paint and you do not want to breathe the airborne ash when it burns off. I put my gloves and mask on, take my tin outside, hold it with the pliers and use a small butane torch to burn the finish off the tin. Have a bucket of cold water handy for quickly cooling off the tin.

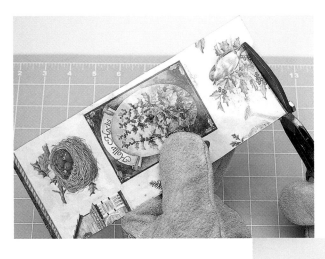
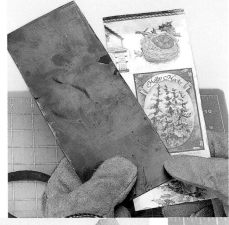

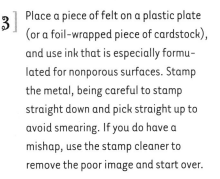

3] Place a piece of felt on a plastic plate (or a foil-wrapped piece of cardstock), and use ink that is especially formulated for nonporous surfaces. Stamp the metal, being careful to stamp straight down and pick straight up to avoid smearing. If you do have a mishap, use the stamp cleaner to remove the poor image and start over.

4] A buildup of permanent ink will harden your stamps, so use permanent ink remover to clean your stamps. I put the cleaner directly onto my stamps and use an old terry cloth rag to wipe them clean.

5] Use the tin snips to cut around the image, leaving a small margin. Wear your work gloves for this step.

6] File the edges of the tin until it is smooth and no longer sharp. Pay close attention to rounding off the corners.

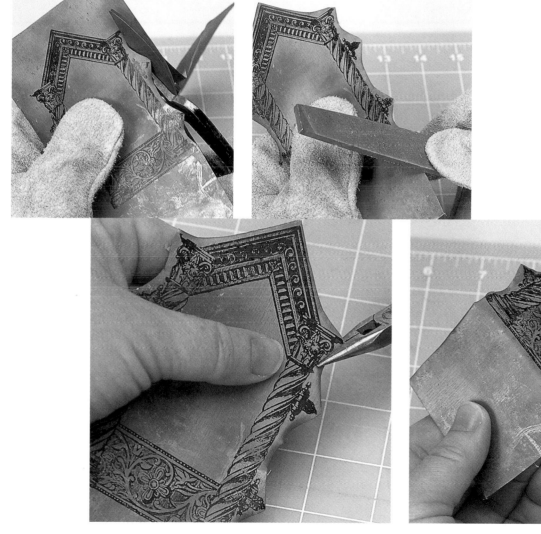

7] Use the pliers to turn the edges under a bit. This will give a nice shape to your sculpture.

8] Hold the tin at the edge of the table and turn it down and to the back to form the stand.

9] Fill a fleur-de-lis with poster tack so that it has a high mound in the center and will have room to expand as you press it onto the tin.

10] Firmly press it onto the tin.

11] **Optional Step:** On this shrine, I used a cork and an awl to punch holes into the tin. These holes can hold earrings for a jewelry stand. They could easily be added decoration for a sculpture.

←←
BROWSE through your trinket drawer and come up with all sorts of objects to make your shrine an interesting and personal art piece. I started with a piece of gold toned metal, stamped and then added a smashed bottle cap, a tile that was stamped with an Acey Deucy image. A few fibers and a touch of wire around a little wooden bead pulled it all together.

→→
THIS is the result of optional step 11. After you punch the holes, you may want to hang earrings as pictured. Another idea would be to make little "S" hooks and hang rings or small trinkets from them. On a larger scale, this would make a great necklace hanger as well.

14 ❧ simply SACHET

SOFT AND SWEETLY SCENTED, a set of elegant sachets makes a thoughtful gift. An architectural stamp combined with creamy mulberry paper and a touch of gold give this packet an old-world charm that is sure to please.

Materials

- *stamps
  (the architectural stamp is from
  Stampers Anonymous and the
  leaves are from Hero Arts)*
- *mulberry paper*
- *coal Ancient Page permanent ink*
- *Clearsnap gold embossing ink
  and powder*
- *cardstock for the leaves*
- *gold cord*
- *felt*
- *scissors
  (plain and decorative)*
- *vanilla potpourri*
- *glue gun*

1] Stamp the mulberry paper with permanent ink.

2] Cut two pieces of felt to make an interior pocket that will hold the potpourri.

3] Using the glue gun, glue three sides of the pocket together. This makes a quick little pocket ready for filling.

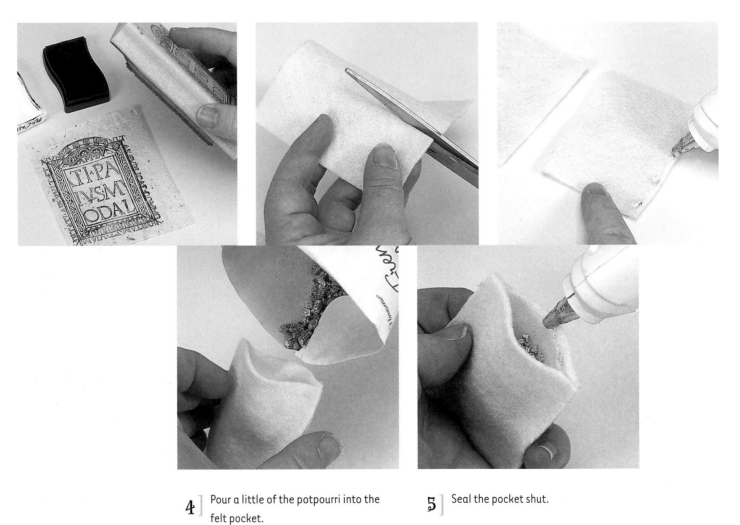

4] Pour a little of the potpourri into the felt pocket.

5] Seal the pocket shut.

6 Place a piece of mulberry paper on the bottom, lay the filled pocket on top and then glue a front piece of mulberry paper onto the whole assembly.

7 For ease of positioning, glue the front mulberry paper to the back paper one side at a time.

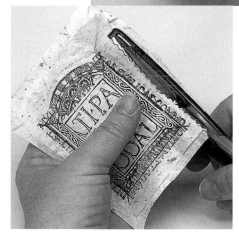

8 Use decorative scissors to edge the sachet. Make three sachets to give as one set.

9 Stamp and emboss the fern leaves. Cut them out.

10 Tie the set together with a pretty gold cord.

15 ☙ Leather NOTEBOOK

AN INTERESTING TWIST to this little notebook is that it has two front covers. One is stamped and cut in the shape of a woman's face that you don't see until you open the book.

The only thing that would make this project any easier would be to take a purchased spiral notebook, remove the spiral wire, make a new cover and reassemble the book. That is a good option if you don't feel like running out to find some wire. Because wire is something that you probably already have on hand, this project is geared to showing you how to make your own spiral. This allows you to make the book any size you want and with any paper.

Materials

- two pieces of smooth leather for the front and back covers (found in most craft stores or through The Leather Factory)
- black permanent inkpad (I used coal Ancient Page)
- stamps (I used stamps from Stamp Oasis)
- textweight paper cut to size [cut it about ¼" (6mm) shorter on the three open sides of the book covers]
- 18-gauge copper wire
- ⅛" (3mm) hole punch
- leather hole punch
- ⅜" (9mm) wooden dowel
- needle-nose pliers
- leather scissors
- watercolor crayons (Staedtler makes a great smooth crayon)
- JudiKins water brush

1️⃣ Cut two leather covers in your desired size and a piece of scrap leather for the face stamp. The covers for my little book are only 2½" x 4" (6cm x 10cm). Stamp your images onto the smooth side of the leather in black permanent ink. (Ancient Page ink comes in several colors and a stamping in color would be as beautiful as black.)

2️⃣ Cut out your image with scissors. I used scissors that are specifically designed for leather and they cut through it easily, but you can use a heavy-duty pair of scissors instead. If you are cutting a lot of leather, I highly recommend getting the leather scissors.

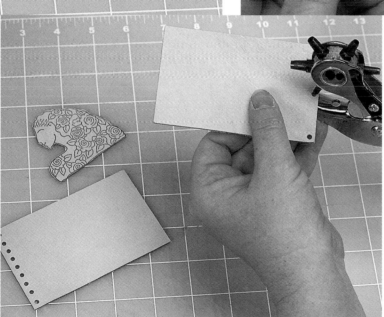

4️⃣ Cut your textweight papers about ⅛" to ¼" (3mm to 6mm) shorter than the leather covers on three sides.

3️⃣ Use the leather punch to punch the holes into each cover. Remember not to go any farther than ¼" (6mm) down or the spiral will not fit the book. If you do punch too far down the page, you will have to get a bigger dowel for a bigger spiral.

　　The photo shows how I determine where to punch the holes, and it is a lot faster than measuring. Punch a hole at either end of the book about ⅛" (3mm) from the spine. Next, estimate where the center is and punch a hole there. Keep punching holes, dividing each space in half as you go.

5] The spiral side will be flush to the cover's edge. Lay a leather cover over the block, mark where the holes should be punched and use the paper punch to punch them.

6] Divide the text block if it is too thick for the paper punch.

7] Lightly color the leather with watercolor crayons.

8] Use a water brush to blend and variegate the crayon colors.

9] Color the front cover. If you don't have time for the watercolors, the leather would look just as good with only the uncolored stamped images.

10] Wrap the wire around the coil two more times than the number of holes that you have punched. In this case, I punched nine holes and then wrapped the wire around the coil eleven times. Snip off the excess wire with your pliers.

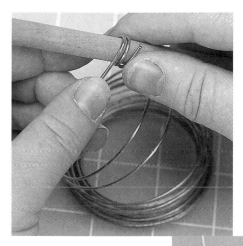

11] Assemble the book: back cover first, then the text block, the front cover and the woman's face.

12] Line up the holes and feed the spiral wire into them, adjusting the wire as you go. If all of the holes are lined up, then the wire will spiral right into place. You will have to adjust the spiral spacing by gently pulling the wire as you feed it into the holes.

13] Use the pliers to shape a curl at both ends of the wire.

16 ⏱ World's Easiest TASSEL

USEFUL FOR SO MANY decorative purposes, a tassel is always a welcome gift. This particular tassel is so easy to make that you will find yourself using the technique repeatedly, either by itself or as an addition to your other crafts. Tassels make great shade or lamp pulls, decorative tiebacks for drapes or dangly embellishments for your wearable art. I only embossed this tassel to make it a fast project, but you can also stamp directly onto the wooden bead or stamp and color a tissue and glue it to the bead.

Materials

- wooden bead with a large hole (the type used for macramé)
- sandpaper
- ¼" (6mm) dowel or pencil
- FolkArt acrylic paints (consider using both the matte and metallic acrylics)
- pigment ink (I used a Petal Point inkpad from Clearsnap)
- copper embossing powder
- heat gun
- fancy fibers
- scrap piece of corrugated or mat board that is the length of tassel you want

OPTIONAL

- gold Krylon gilding pen or a black Sharpie marker

1] Lightly sand the bead to remove the shine.

2] Slide the bead onto a pencil or a dowel and dab acrylic paint onto the bead in a pretty, random manner. Do this lightly so the paint will dry quickly.

3] Randomly dab pigment ink over the bead, being careful not to entirely cover the acrylic paint. Sprinkle embossing powder on the bead and shake off the excess.

4] Use the heat gun to melt the embossing powder.

6 Cut slits at the end of the corrugated board. Slip the ends of the fibers into one slit and wrap the fancy fibers around the board until the bunch is thick enough to fit into the bead hole securely. Cut off and secure the ends in the second slit.

5 **Optional Step**: Color the ends of the bead with a gold pen, paint or a black Sharpie.

7 Slip a length of cord under the wrapped fibers and tie it off at the end with a simple slip knot. (I made my own cord from braided fibers, but you can save time by using a purchased cord.)

8 Slide the knot around and under the top of the wrapped fibers to hide it in the tassel head.

9 Tie another knot at the top of the tassel as close to the wrapped fibers as you can get. Slide the wrapped fiber bunch off the corrugated board.

10 Slip the tassel tie through the bead, carefully pulling it up to fit.

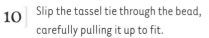

11 Trim the ends of the tassel.

WITH a little extra time, you can stamp directly onto the bead with an embossing ink, sprinkle the embossing powder, tap off the excess, and heat.

17 ⏱ Carved Ivory BRACELET

LET'S MAKE OLD IVORY!

You will love the results of this technique. It is a very delicate "carved ivory" made from shrink plastic. Add this imitative effect to beads and wire for a unique wearable. The project pictured in the step by steps takes a little longer because it is more involved. The bracelet pictured here is a variation that is less time-consuming to make (more details on page 83).

Materials

- rubber stamps with an open design (I used ones from Hero Arts)
- Crafter's ink in various colors
- chalk in various colors
- white shrink plastic
- template on page 121
- ⅛" (3mm) hole punch or pin vise
- permanent marker
- medium-grit sandpaper
- heat gun

- drill bit or knife (anything to scratch lines into the plastic)
- 20-gauge wire
- little beads, two jump rings and a bracelet closure
- needle-nose pliers
- Crafter's Pick The Ultimate glue or a cyanoacrylate glue like Zap-a-Gap

OPTIONAL

- scissors and pinking sheers

1] Cut out the pattern and use it to trace (using a black permanent marker) the base rectangular shape on white shrink plastic. Then cut out seven of these shapes (or six or eight depending on your wrist size).

2] Punch holes into the plastic. If you forget to punch the holes before you shrink the plastic, use the pin vise (pictured in the next step) and drill holes into it after shrinking.

3] Run the sandpaper across the plastic in one direction to create random stripes. Use the pin vise or your knife to scratch a few bigger stripes into the plastic. You are trying to simulate the grain of ivory or bone, so make the stripes more dense in some areas and less so in others.

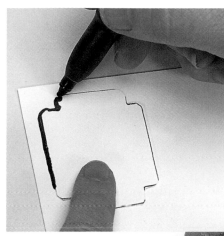

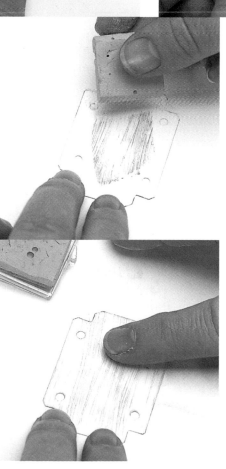

5] Use Crafter's ink to color the edges and top of the plastic. The plastic will shrink, condensing the color, so use light colors of ink and chalks. The Crafter's ink will be permanent after you heat set it in the shrinking process.

4] Brush chalk across the plastic and press it in with your fingers. Use a variety of browns and tans.

6] Shrink the plastic with your heat gun.

7] When the plastic stops shrinking, use a piece of acrylic (or something else) to flatten it. Let the plastic cool for a couple of seconds, then remove the acrylic. You can use the sandpaper to burnish off a little color if you want. If you want to darken the piece, add more Crafter's ink, reheat and reflatten.

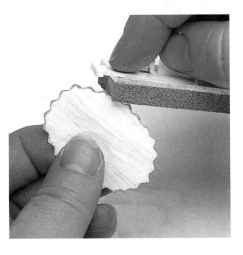

8] Cut an oval about ⅛" (3mm) smaller than the rectangle on all sides. I used the pinking shears to cut these in a freehand manner. Don't worry about having an imperfect oval. When the plastic shrinks and you stamp into it, the edges will be irregular anyway.

Use the sandpaper, chalks and inks to texture and color the oval as you did for the rectangle. Remember to color the edges of the plastic with Crafter's ink. If you don't, they will smash out when you stamp into the hot plastic, revealing stark white edges.

9] Heat the plastic as you did before, but this time, when the plastic has stopped shrinking, bring the gun in close to get it hot. Press your stamp on it firmly, cool a few seconds, then remove the plastic from the stamp.

10 Use sandpaper to remove color from the raised areas and bring a little of the white plastic into view. This will high-light your "carving."

11 Glue the oval piece to the rectangular piece. If the top oval is a little large and covers the holes, you can trim the edges with a pair of scissors.

12 Use the pliers to form a loop at one end of the wire, slip a bead on and form the loop at the other end for connectors between the plastic pieces.

13 Assemble the bracelet.

← **FASTER!** If you don't have much time, you can skip making the beaded wire connections by purchasing a blank linked bracelet at a bead store. Then glue the plastic directly onto the metal bracelet.

18 ⊙ Ice Maiden PIN

YES, SHE IS a maiden!

For some reason, everyone keeps calling this image a guy. Can't you see her little hooded snow sweater with the pattern across the front and her oh-so-chic ski pants? All right, so I am not so sure why there are wings on an ice maiden except that maybe skiing makes her feel like she is flying! To make this pin project go more quickly, I stamped the maiden onto commercially printed fabric.

Materials

- stamp (I used a Gains & McCall from Stamp Oasis)
- fabric and felt
- fabric glue
- heat gun or iron
- scissors
- black Crafter's ink and an assortment of colors
- colored pencils
- black permanent fine-line pen
- metal wings
- pin back

OPTIONAL
- hot foil pen
- JudiKins Roxs
- little beads or other jewelry findings

1 | Use black Crafter's ink to stamp an image onto printed fabric. **Important note** (this step is not pictured): Set the Crafter's ink with a heat gun. You could also use an iron, but you *must* heat set this ink before you go on to the next step.

2 | Add colored Crafter's ink. Use colored pencils to add more color if you like. Heat set the Crafter's ink when you are satisfied with your coloring job. Cut out the stamped image, leaving a margin of about ³⁄₈" (10mm) all around.

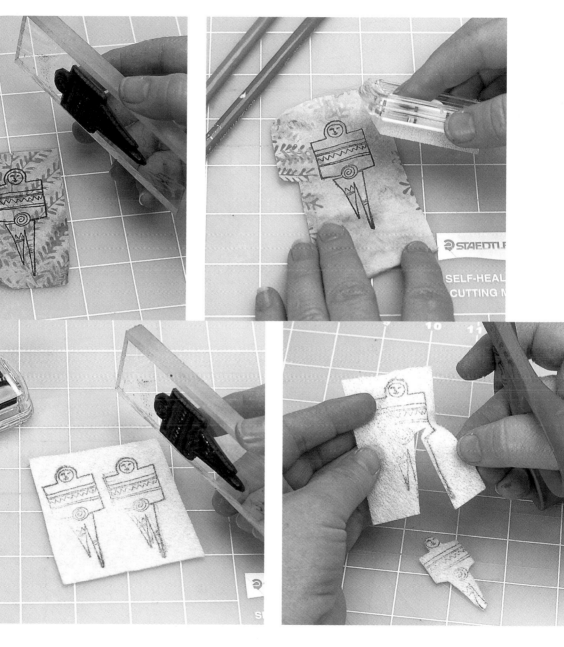

3 | Stamp twice onto felt using the black ink.

4 | Cut one piece of felt about ¹⁄₁₆" (2mm) inside the stamped outline. Cut another piece that is about ¹⁄₈" (3mm) inside the outline of the stamped image.

5 Put a small drop of glue between the layers to tack them together. The smallest felt will go next to the back side of your stamped and colored fabric, and then the larger felt will go on top of that.

6 Put the fabric glue all around the outside margin, from the felt to the fabric edges.

7 Lay your fabric backing face side down. Position the pin on top and press the edges down, forming a puffy shape as you go.

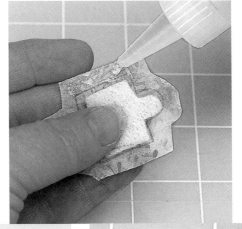

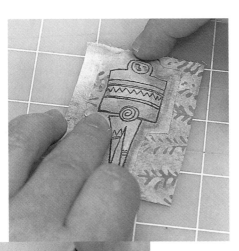

8 Cut around the pin, leaving about a ⅛" (3mm) margin. Cut through the glued edges to keep the pin from fraying.

9 Use a permanent pen to add detail to the stamped image.

1   Stamp the image in coal Ancient Page or black permanent ink on the smooth side of the leather. (Ancient Page ink comes in several other colors and a stamping in color would be beautiful as well.)

2   Cut out the image with heavy-duty or leather scissors.

3   Color the edge with a permanent marker.

4   For expediency, use a glue gun to attach the barrette finding to the leather. For longevity, use good glue that will stick to metals, such as Fabri-Tac or Crafter's Pick The Ultimate glue. When you use glues to attach barrettes or pin backs that have those small holes in them, let a little of the glue leak through and form a bead. Do not wipe that away. Let it dry in a nice little round ball and it will help hold the metal backing to your project.

↑ IF you have a little extra time, consider using pigment ink and embossing powders, or using the metallic colors or even watercolors over your permanent ink. Also consider using other base materials. This barrette has been cut out of chipboard, stamped, embossed, and then wrapped with a copper foil and self-adhesive tape. Use a bone folder or the end of a pen to burnish the foiled edges.

21 · Leather PIN

WHETHER gilded, glazed or just stamped and painted, this project pin will add casual elegance to your outfit. For other pins, keep your stamped image simple and in a design that can be cut and assembled into at least three layers. If you have more time, think about tucking in fibers, wires and beads so they cleverly peek out from between the layers.

Materials

- piece of stiff leather
- sun and stars stamp (from Stamp Oasis)
- coal Ancient Page permanent ink
- sharp scissors
- leather glue or clear-drying glue
- leather sheen
- Staedtler watercolor crayons

- JudiKins water brush
- pin back
- glue gun

OPTIONAL

- Staedtler hot foil pen
- foil
- Diamond Glaze

1 Stamp the leather with coal Ancient Page permanent ink for three images.

2 Use sharp scissors to cut out the images. Cut one as a full image, which will be the pin backing. Cut another as just the sun and stars, which will be the second layer. Cut the round part of the sun for the third and top layer.

3 Use leather glue or a clear-drying white glue to assemble the pin. If you coat both pieces with the leather glue and use it like contact cement, you will get a great bond—much better than you would with regular white glue. Be sure not to get excess glue on the piece or the watercolor will not stick. If you do get excess glue on the leather, use the water brush to clean it away before it dries.

4 Color the piece with watercolor crayons. Of course, regular watercolors will work too, but I want you to see how easy and fun it is to work with these crayons. You don't even have to do a good color job. What could be easier?

5 Use the water brush to smooth and blend the crayon color. Again, the water brush is just a fun option. A regular brush and a cup of water would also work, but this water brush is very convenient, especially if you are traveling or have a large class and don't want to bother with all those water cups.

7] For speed, use a glue gun to attach the pin back. If you have extra time for the glue to dry, Fabri-Tac works great for attaching pin backs. It dries flexible and will not pop off like some glue. Remember to let a little dot of glue ooze up through the holes in the pin backs. This will help to keep it better attached no matter what kind of glue you use.

6] Coat the pin with a spray of leather sheen.

8] **Optional Step:** For added pizzazz, use Diamond Glaze. Only apply it to the higher layers and it will really make them stand out.

 THIS pin has been further embellished with a gold Krylon pen. You may also want to use the awl to punch a hole at the bottom of the pin on which to hang charms.

9] **Optional Step:** Another option is to use the foil pen to add a dash of golden highlights.

➡ **FOR** this pin, cutting the Rubbermoon image in threes puts the face as the top layer. Tucking a few fibers behind the crown gives the pin extra punch. Notice I did not waste time cutting around the little detail ribbon of the original stamped image on the top layer.

22 ❀ Copper Leaves PIN

THOUGH QUITE different

from each other, the design

elements—rustic tin, shiny brass

charms and tiny beads—work

together to create magic. The

sprinkling of colored embossing

powder breaks up the expanse of rusted tin to

give this pin a warm and timeless quality.

Materials

- rusted tin leaves
- needle-nose pliers
- heat gun
- embossing powders (fall colors)
- embossing ink
- little gold beads
- gold leaf charms
- pin back
- clear-drying white glue (I used Crafter's Pick The Ultimate glue)
- glue gun

1] Use the pliers to shape the rusted tin leaves.

2] Randomly dab embossing ink over the leaf.

3] Sprinkle various embossing powders over the leaf.

4] Heat the embossing powder with the gun. Do not forget to hold the metal with pliers, tongs or something other than your fingers. The metal gets very hot.

5] Use clear-drying white glue to attach the tiny beads and charms to the embossed leaf.

6] If you have time, Fabri-Tac is a good quick-drying glue for the pin backs. If you're in a hurry, a glue gun will work.

23 ❧ NYLON BRACELET

A TRUE CONVERSATION PIECE, this bracelet features stamped art under glass with slip knot ties on either end. A variety of fabulous designs and textures are available in woven ribbons of all types. If you pick a ribbon made of nylon, then you can make a simple, finished end by melting it. With a decidedly American Indian motif, this particular ribbon from The Leather Factory has a comfortable weight and is flexible but holds a good shape.

Materials

- nylon ribbon
- black waxed cord
- clear, flat glass marbles (found in floral departments of craft stores)
- stamps (from Acey Deucy, Inkadinkado and Stamp Oasis)
- white gloss cardstock
- black Ancient Page permanent ink
- clear-drying white glue (Crafter's Pick The Ultimate glue holds glass marbles very well)
- awl and cork
- heat source to melt the ends of the cord

1 | Stamp onto white cardstock with black permanent ink.

2 | Cut the stamped art into circles and glue them to the back of the glass marbles with clear-drying white glue.

3 | Cut the cord to the size of your wrist. Use a lighter to melt the ends for a smooth finish. You could certainly fold and glue the ends under if you do not want to melt them.

4 | Set the bracelet on a cork and punch a hole through the ends for the cord ties.

5 | Fold a thin, waxed cord in half and slip it into the hole for the ties. You may need to use a pencil or awl to push the cord into the hole. Make a tie at each end of the bracelet.

6 | Use clear-drying white glue to attach the marble art onto the bracelet. For spacing, glue the middle marble first, then the end marbles. Place the other two marbles in the middle of the remaining space on either side of the bracelet.

24 snappy CLIP

EYE-CATCHING

and fun, these little whim-

sies are just a stamp and an

inking away from a cultural

revolution. OK, maybe I shouldn't

go that far, but they are different!

Don't think of them as just hair ornaments. And

they are not just for kids either. They are great when clipped to

your lapel, your hat or even your belt.

Materials

- *felt-covered clips*
- *stamps [the faces are from Zettiology Rubber Stamps & Mythos (Teesha Moore)]*
- *black permanent ink and straw dye ink*
- *colored Crafter's ink*
- *Color Dusters or a stipple brush*
- *colored pencils*
- *clear, flat glass marble*
- *little beads and yarns for embellishment*
- *clear-drying white glue (I used Crafter's Pick The Ultimate glue)*
- *scissors*
- *toothpick*
- *mist bottle*

1] You can buy these felt-covered clips at almost any beauty supply store. They are usually packaged twelve to a card and are very inexpensive.

2] Don't worry about the color of the felt. You can use your Crafter's inks to color them as you like. I prefer muted colors, so I start by misting the felt. Tap different colors of ink onto the felt clip, misting as you go. Set them aside to dry and go onto the stamping.

3] Stamp your image in black permanent ink. Stipple dye ink color onto your image.

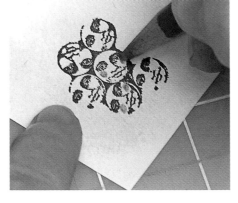

4] Add color with colored pencils if you prefer.

5] Cut out the stamped and colored images.

6 Use a clear-drying white glue to attach
the stamped images to the back of a
marble. Glue that to the felt clip.

7 Use a toothpick to glue the fiber and
the little beads into place.

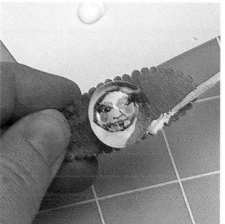

25 Versatile MOTIF

A SPIN off the Ice Maiden Pin (see page 84), this very versatile fabric motif can be made into a pin, an element for assemblage or a charming addition to a gift tag. Stamping on commercially colored fabric with no additional detail coloring makes it easy and fast. A glue gun also adds to the speedy nature of this project and will hold the fabric just fine.

Materials

- *stamp (I used one from Postmodern Design)*
- *fabric*
- *cardstock*
- *cotton balls*
- *glue gun or fabric glue*
- *scissors*
- *black Crafter's ink*

- *heat gun or iron*
- *little beads in assorted colors*
- *heavy-duty thread (I used waxed linen beading thread)*

OPTIONAL
- *Fray Check*

1] Use black Crafter's ink to stamp an image on printed fabric. Heat set the ink with a heat gun or an iron.

2] Cut out the stamped image. An option (as shown) is to fray the edges of the motif to add interest and textural appeal.

3] If you do not want the edges to fray, put Fray Check all the way around your cutout and let it dry.

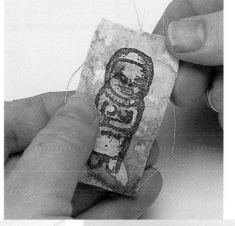

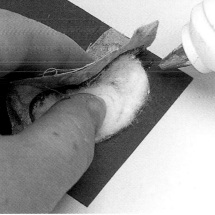

4] Glue two sides of the fabric motif face up on the cardstock. Tuck in a cotton ball and glue the other edges down.

5] Undercut the cardstock so that the fabric extends beyond the cardstock edges.

6] Snip little divots into the cardstock and fabric here and there.

7] Feed a few beads onto your thread. Do not cut the thread off the spool at this point.

 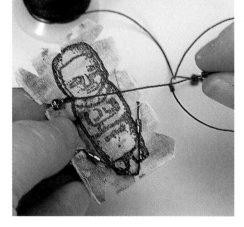 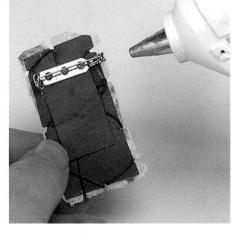

8] After you are satisfied with the amount of beads you have threaded, tie a knot at the beginning of the thread, leaving a little tail about 1" (2.5cm) long. Secure the knot in one of the divots.

9] Wrap the beaded thread around the assembly, moving the beads to the front of the motif as you go.

10] When you have enough wraps, cut the thread from the spool and secure the ends with a patch of cardstock and glue.

CUT a piece of decorative paper to make this gift tag. Layer the paper onto colored coordinated cardstock and glue the motif into place. You can write "To" and "From" information on the back of the card. The gift wrap pictured here has been monoprinted, and stamped.

IN your collage box, you may have cards that looked great as backgrounds but just didn't work well by themselves. Adding one of these little motifs to the center of the card can pull the whole assembly together. The center panel of the card has been stamped twice with an image from Postmodern Design with an off-set look. For the border background card, I've used Clearsnap's idea of tapping white pigment ink all over a white card. Then I used a sponge stylus tip to drag a darker pigment ink through the white. The border images from Hero Arts are stamped in the dark ink and the card was finally embossed with clear powder.

TRY an assemblage when you have a little time for rummaging. While not for a quick gift, this is a great way to use your motifs in a more substantial way. Here, a variety of trinkets were painted and glued to a background card that was embossed with pigment inks. The motif holds its place as the center of attention

26 ✦ Winged PIN

THIS PIN is a simpler version of one of my best-sellers. It is elegant and funky-cool at the same time, so it makes a nice gift for all ages. The time-consuming part was in the original design. Now that you have all the specifics, it will not take you any time at all to make.

If you need to make several of these pins, reproduce and multiply the pattern onto a sheet of sticker paper or white cardstock. Stamp over the copied patterns, spray mount it to the chipboard and cut out all of your bodies at one time. Continue to work in assembly-line fashion and you will have several pins after just a few hours of work. If you have extra time and want to make a more substantial pin, look for the special notes in the instructions.

Materials

- stamp
  (I used one from Stamp Oasis)
- black inkpad
- white cardstock or white sticker paper
- template on page 121
- thin chipboard
- clear, self-sticking label material
- copper adhesive-backed foil tape

- copper Krylon gilding pen
- glue
- butterfly hair clip
- pliers or tongs
- mask
- bone folder or Sharpie marker
- ⅛" (3mm) hole punch
- metal file
- fire source
- key or other charm

- jump ring
- head pin
- bead dangle
- pin back
- glue gun
- scissors

OPTIONAL

- Silver/Black and a cotton swab for aging

1 Use the template to trace the base shape onto white cardstock. Stamp a text image with black ink. **Note:** I have traced two shapes on the cardstock and stamped over them to show you that you can make extras with just one stamping. I usually do multiple stampings to save time. That way, I have more pin bodies ready to go when I need them.

2 Use a quick-drying glue or spray-mount adhesive to adhere the stamped cardstock to the chipboard.

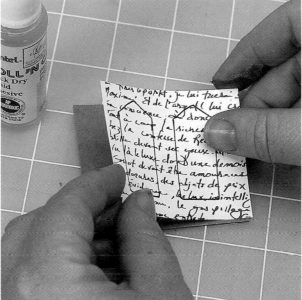

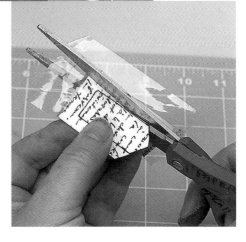

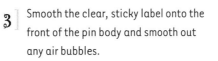

3 Smooth the clear, sticky label onto the front of the pin body and smooth out any air bubbles.

4 Trim to the pointed, rectangular shape of the template.

tip

Use a thin, clear styrene to achieve a more substantial body. **Styrene** can be cut with scissors, so it is easy to use. It is readily available through hobby or plastics stores.

5] Use the copper gilding pen to color the chipboard pin backing.

6] Wrap adhesive-backed foil tape all around the pin body. Clip the corners and turn down the edges of the tape.

7] Use a bone folder or the cap of a Sharpie to burnish the kinks out of the copper tape.

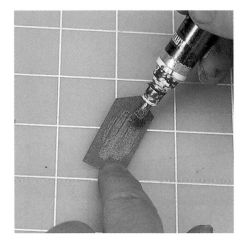

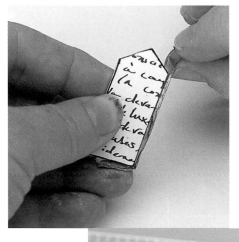

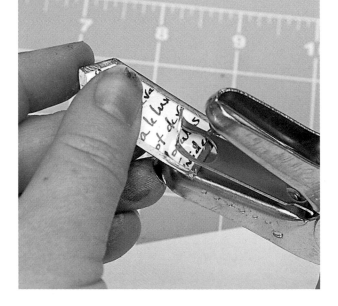

tips

If you have time to go shopping, look for a backing sheet of **real copper** to glue to the chipboard. This will take the pin into the classy realm. Copper sheeting can be found in most stamp stores.

For an aged look, you can use a cotton swab and a product called **Silver/Black**. Just dip the swab and "paint" the copper. It will darken and add a lot of beauty to the final product.

If you use a heavier plastic such as styrene or acrylic, you will need to **drill the hole** into the pin body instead of punching it.

8] Use a ⅛" (3mm) hole punch to punch a hole through the bottom of the assembly.

10 Hold the wings with tongs or a pair of pliers and burn off the glittery finish. This will age them and give a pretty patina to the metal. During the photography, we used a fire starter. This works, but it takes longer to burn off the glitter. I use a torch and work outside, stringing the clips onto a metal stand to make the work go faster.

9 Pull the wings off the butterfly hair clip.

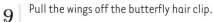

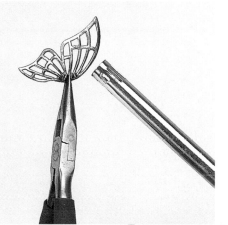

11 Pull any excess metal off the wings and use a metal file to sand off any rough edges.

12 For speed, use a glue gun to attach the pin backs. For longevity (and if you have the drying time), opt for a glue such as Quick Grab, E6000, Crafter's Pick The Ultimate glue or Fabri-Tac.

13 Glue the pin back on the upper part of the pin. Remember that if you glue the pin back too far down, it will flop forward when you wear it.

14 To make a dangle, load a head pin with beads. Use your cutters to snip off the end, leaving about ³⁄₈" (9mm) to work with. Put the pliers close to the last bead and bend the pin at a right angle.

15 Use the pliers to grasp the end of the head pin. Turn your wrist upward for a quarter turn. Move the pliers down a bit and turn upward for another quarter turn.

16 Repeat until you have wound the pin back onto itself, making a centered circle closure.

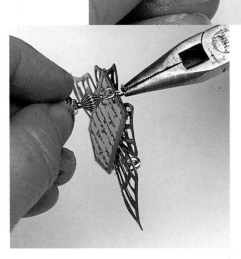

17 Attach the dangle to the pin with a jump ring.

18 Use your knife to score hash marks into the plastic.

19 Glue the charm to the front of the pin.

27 ⏱ Wooden Heart PIN

A GLITTERING halo of gold dust encircles this stunningly simple pin. Details such as the colored pencil work and embossing belie the quick artistry of this project. If you do not have the extra twenty minutes to wait for the Diamond Glaze to dry, you can easily substitute a glossy spray sealant for a shiny finish.

Materials

- ◆ wooden heart
- ◆ three women stamp (from Stamp Oasis)
- ◆ coal Ancient Page permanent ink
- ◆ Diamond Glaze
- ◆ colored pencils
- ◆ embossing pen
- ◆ gold embossing powder
- ◆ pliers
- ◆ heat gun
- ◆ pin back
- ◆ glue gun or quick-drying glue

1] Stamp the image in coal permanent ink.

2] Color the image with pencils, using a cream pencil to blend.

3] Color the edge of the heart with an embossing pen.

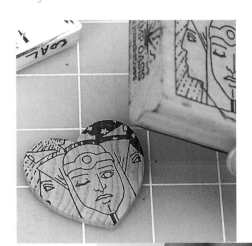

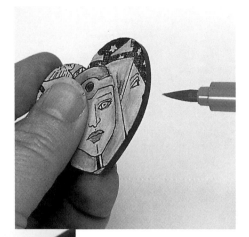

4] Dip the pin into gold embossing powder.

5] Hold the heart with a pair of pliers and emboss the pin. Remember that wood gets hotter than paper, so you need to wait a few seconds to let it cool before you touch it.

6 Squeeze a small amount of Diamond Glaze on the heart and use your fingers to spread it around evenly.

7 It is better to build up a couple of light layers of Diamond Glaze rather than lay down one heavy layer. A heavy layer will dry milky on the pin.

8 Use the glue gun or quick-drying glue to set the pin back. Remember to set it high on the wood so the pin will not flop forward when you wear it.

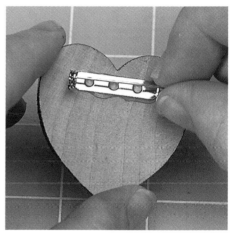

A FEW time-saving steps were used on this pin. I skipped the gold embossing and, instead, used a gold pen for edging. A spray sealant was used on this pin and then it was sealed with a fast-drying clear nail polish. I did have to put two coats of polish on the pin to build up the gloss.

GALLERY

➡➡

DÉCOUPAGED BEADS Stamp onto tissue paper with a black permanent inkpad like Ancient Page ink. Cut out and glue to a wooden bead with Diamond Glaze or Dimensional magic. If you slip the bead onto a pencil, it will be easier to handle. Keep your fingers wet with glaze while you glue and smooth the tissue onto the bead. This will coat the bead with glaze at the same time that you glue it.

After the glaze has dried, use a Color Duster to stipple color onto the bead. I used Ancient Page in Saffron and Sienna. That way it dries permanent even over the glaze and doesn't have to be sealed. The ends of these beads have been coated with a black Sharpie. STAMPS: BLACK CAT DESIGN, HERO ARTS, POSTMODERN DESIGN AND STAMPA ROSA.

⚓ FAUX PAPIER MÂCHÉ BOWLS

Stamp onto mulberry paper with acrylic paint. Tear the paper into strips and glue onto a paper picnic bowl with watered-down white glue. You can add additional stamping and embossing directly to the bowl after the glue is dry. If you have extra time, try sewing fibers around the top for an interesting look. STAMPS: CLEARSNAP AND HERO ARTS.

GLUE STICK NAPKIN RING Cut a piece of foamcore board to the size of a stamp. Squeeze a mound of glue stick from a glue gun onto the foamcore board. Ink the stamp with embossing ink and then stamp into the hot glue. Pull the stamp off the glue when it has cooled. Paint with metallic acrylics and embellish with the tiny gold beads. Glue the medallion onto a piece of wrapped paper, fabric or cording. STAMPS: STAMP OASIS. HANDMADE PAPER: LOOSE ENDS.

STAMPED NAPKIN Buy inexpensive napkins [or make them by cutting a 15" (38cm) square of fabric and fraying the edges as I have done here] and stamp across two ends with black Crafter's ink. Heat set with an iron. STAMP: BLACK CAT DESIGN.

COVERED NOTEPAD Cut two chipboard covers a little larger than the notepad on three sides. Stamp onto the chipboard if you like. Place one piece of chipboard on the front of the pad and one on the back. Tape the assembly together with a black fabric tape. Decorate the chipboard covers with a collage of stamped and cut out images.
STAMPS: STAMP FRANCISCO AND DENAMI.

TYVEK BEADS Ink two stamps with embossing ink and set aside. Cut a square of Tyvek (I use the Tyvek mailing envelopes) about 4" x 4" (10cm x 10cm). Skewer it onto an awl that has been coated with embossing ink. Melt it with your heat gun until it forms a little ball around your awl. You may need to form it a little with the tip of your scissors. Place the wad of Tyvek, with the awl still in it, on one of the face-up stamps. Bring the other stamp down on top and hold for a few seconds. The Tyvek gets very hot, so wait until it cools to remove it from the rubber stamps and twist it off the awl. Paint with metallic acrylics.

STYRENE AND VELVET PINS Stamp woman's face onto white cardstock. Stipple a base coat of Vivid straw ink and then color with pencils. Glue to a piece of chipboard and then cut into a circular shape. Cut a piece of styrene or acetate and layer it on top of the stamped face. Sandwich the layers together with copper tape, burnish it flat and use liver of sulfur to antique the tape. Use a glue gun to attach colorful velvet leaves plus other embellishments like tinsel, berries, or pretty ribbons. Attach a pin back. STAMP: HANDMADE, WITH FACE FROM DOVER CLIP ART.

TEMPLATES

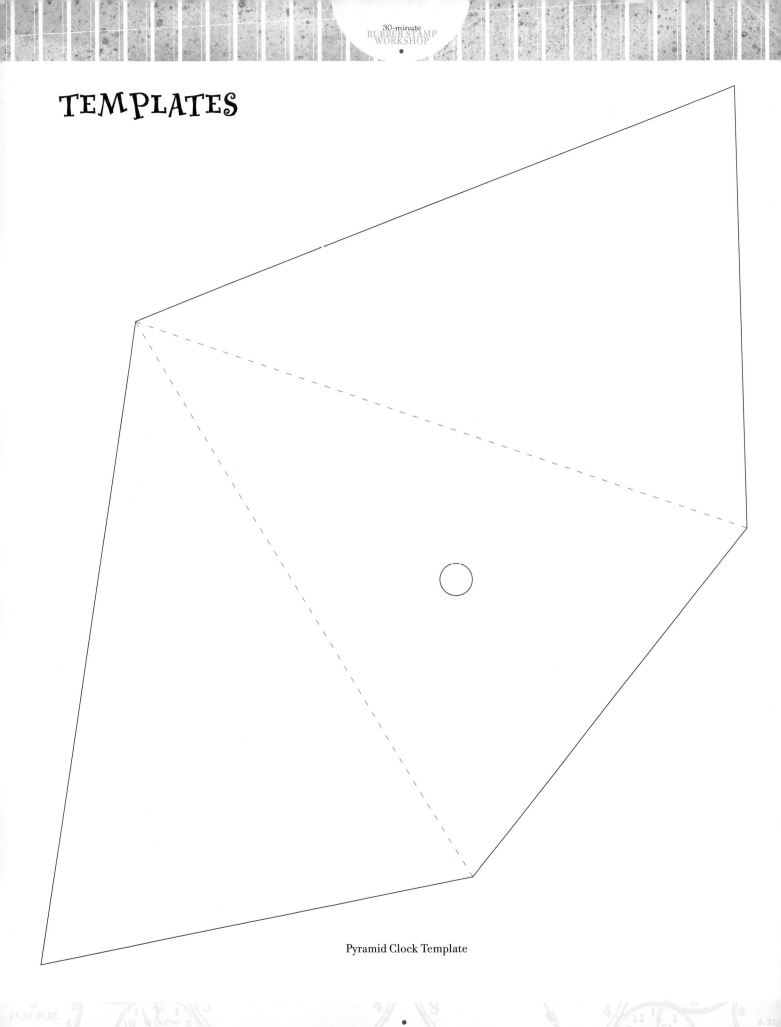

Pyramid Clock Template

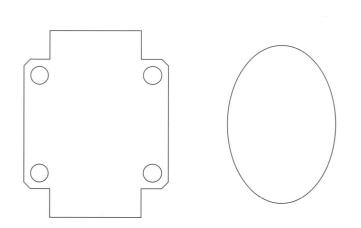

Carved Ivory Bracelet Template

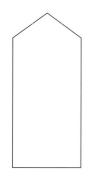

Winged Pin Template

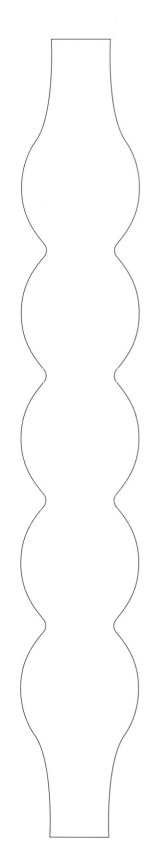

Leather Band Template

RESOURCES

☺ Favorite Stamp Companies

Acey Deucy
P.O. Box 194
Ancram, NY 12502
www.stampdiva.com/aceydeucy.html

**All Night Media /
Plaid Enterprises**
(see Plaid Enterprises)

American Art Stamp
3870 Del Amo Blvd., Ste. 501
Torrance, CA 90503
www.americanartstamp.com

Anima Designs
P.O. Box 91385
Pittsburgh, PA 15221-7385
(800) 570-6847
www.animadesigns.com

A Stamp in the Hand Co.
20507 S. Belshaw Ave.
Carson, CA 90746
(310) 884-9700
www.astampinthehand.com

Black Cat Creations
P.O. Box 489
Everton Park QLD 4053
Australia

Claudia Rose
15 Baumgarten
Saugerties, NY 12477
http://hometown.aol.com/claudirose

Comotion
(see Uptown Design Company)

DeNami Design
P.O. Box 5617
Kent, WA 98064
(253) 437-1626
www.denamidesign.com

Ducks in a Row
323 E. Matilija #110-177
Ojai, CA 93023
http://ducks.htmlbook.com

ERA Graphics
1705 Big Oak Rd.
Placerville, CA 95667
(530) 344-9322
www.eragraphics.com

Hero Arts
1343 Powell St.
Emeryville, CA 94608
(800) 822-4376
www.heroarts.com

Impress Me
17116 Escalon Dr.
Encino, CA 91436-4030
www.impressmenow.com

Inkadinkado Rubber Stamps
61 Holton St.
Woburn, MA 01801
(800) 888-4652
www.inkadinkado.com

JudiKins
17803 S. Harvard Blvd.
Gardena, CA 90248
www.judikins.com

Magenta Rubber Stamps
2275 Bombardier
Sainte-Julie, Quebec J3E 2J9 Canada
(450) 922-5253
www.magentarubberstamps.com

Paper Parachute
P.O. Box 91385
Portland, OR 97291-0385
(503) 533-4513
www.paperparachute.com

Personal Stamp Exchange (PSX)
360 Sutton Pl.
Santa Rosa, CA 95407
(800) 782-6748
www.psxdesign.com

Posh Impressions
22600-A Lambert St., Ste 706
Lake Forest, CA 92630
(800) 421-7674
www.poshimpressions.com

Postmodern Design
P.O. Box 720416
Norman, OK 73070
(405) 321-3176
(405) 321-2296 fax

Postscript Studios
P.O. Box 1539
Placentia, CA 92871
www.postscriptstudios.com

Rubber Monger
P.O. Box 1777
Snowflake, AZ 85937-1777
(928) 536-5128
www.rubbermonger.com

Supplies

Rubbermoon Stamp Company
P.O. Box 3258
Hayden Lake, ID 83835
www.rubbermoon.com

Rubber Stampede
2550 Pellissier Pl.
Whittier, CA 90601
(800) 423-4135
www.deltacrafts.com/RubberStampede

Stampa Rosa, Inc.
60 Maxwell Ct.
Santa Rosa, CA 95401
(800) 554-5755
www.stamparosa.com

Stampendous!
1240 N. Red Gum
Anaheim, CA 92806-1820
(800) 869-0474
www.stampendous.com

Stampers Anonymous
(The Creative Block)
Williamsburg Square
25967 Detroit Rd.
Westlake, OH 44145
(440) 250-9112
www.stampersanonymous.com

Stampington & Company
22992 Mill Creek, Ste. B
Laguna Hills, CA 92653
(877) STAMPER
www.stampington.com

Stamp Oasis
4750 W. Sahara Ave., Ste. 17
Las Vegas, NV 89102
(702) 878-6474
www.stampoasis.com

Stephanie Olin's Designs
6171 Foxshield Dr.
Huntington Beach, CA 92647
(714) 848-1227
www.stephanieolin.com

Time to Stamp
P.O. Box 839
Beaumont, CA 92223-0839
(909) 845-9242
www.timetostamp.com

Tin Can Mail
(see Stampa Rosa, Inc.)

Uptown Design Company
1000 Town Center, Ste. 1
Browns Point, WA 98422
www.uptowndesign.com

Zettiology Rubber Stamps &
Mythos (Teesha Moore)
P.O. Box 3329
Renton, WA 98056
(425) 888-3191
www.zettiology.com

ZimPrints Rubber Stamps
7121 Merrick Drive SW
Knoxville, TN 37919-8119
(865) 584-9430
www.zimprints.com

Beacon Adhesives Company Inc.
125 MacQuesten Parkway South
Mt. Vernon, NY 10550
(914) 699-3400
www.beacon1.com
- *Fabri-Tac glue*

Clearsnap
P.O. Box 98
Anacortes, WA 98221
(888) 448-4862
www.clearsnap.com
- *pens, inks, stamps and lots of other fun stuff*

Fiskars
7811 W. Stewart Ave.
Wausau, WI 54401
(800) 950-0203
www.fiskars.com
- *scissors and paper cutters*

Kelly Paper
1441 E. 16th St.
Los Angeles, CA 90021
(800) 675-3559
www.kellypaper.com
- *paper products*

The Leather Factory
P.O. Box 50429
Ft. Worth, Texas 76105
(800) 433-3201
www.leatherfactory.com
- *specialty, garment and other leathers*

Loose Ends LLC
2065 Madrona Ave., SE
Salem, OR 97302
(503) 390-2348
www.looseends.com
- *handmade papers and tin garlands*

Lucky Squirrel

P.O. Box 606

Belen, NM 87002

(800) 462-4912

www.luckysquirrel.com

- *shrink plastic*

Papers by Catherine

11328 S. Post Oak #108

Houston, TX 77035

(713) 723-3334

www.papersbycatherine.com

- *handmade and decorative paper*

Pentel of America, LTD.

2805 Columbia St.

Torrance, CA 90509

(310) 320-3831

http://www.pentel.com/4prod.html

- *rolling glue and pens*

Plaid Enterprises

3225 Westech

Norcross, GA 30092

(800) 842-4197

www.plaidonline.com

- *acrylic paints, All Night Media stamps and lots of other fun craft stuff*

Polyform Products

1901 Estes Ave.

Elk Grove Village, IL 60007

www.sculpey.com

- *polymer clay*

Quick Grab

242 Neck Rd.

Haverhill, MA 01835

(978) 374-0094

www.quickgrab.com

- *Quick Grab® adhesive*

Ranger Industries, Inc.

15 Park Rd.

Tinton Falls, NJ 07724

(800) 244-2211

www.rangerink.com

- *inkpads, embossing powders and more*

Staedtler

21900 Plummer St.

Chatsworth, CA 91311

www.staedtler-usa.com

- *crayons, markers, pencils, cutting mats, carving blocks, etc.*

Suze Weinberg Design Studio

11 Bannard St.

Freehold, NJ 07728

(732) 761-2406

www.schmoozewithsuze.com

- *Ultra Thick Embossing Enamel and more*

Think Ink

322 NE 162nd

Shoreline, WA 98155

(800) 778-1935

www.thinkink.net

- *embossing powders*

Tsukineko, Inc.

17640 NE 65th St.

Redmond, WA 98052

(800) 769-6633

www.tsukineko.com

- *pens and inks*

USArtQuest, Inc.

7800 Ann Arbor Rd.

Grass Lake, MI 49240

(800) 200-7848

www.usartquest.com

- *Perfect Paper Adhesive™*

VIP (Visual Image Printery)

1215 N. Grove St.

Anaheim, CA 92806

(800) 8-VISUAL

www.bentopoint.com/Pages/vipsample1.htm

- *foils and spray webbing*

Woodworks, LTD.

4521 Anderson Blvd.

Fort Worth, TX 76117

(800) 722-0311

www.woodwrks.com

- *wooden items of all types*

Where I get my drawing and carvings turned into rubber stamps:

Rand'M Engraving & Distributing

15906 Rinaldi St.

Granada Hills, CA 91344

(818) 360-6016

http://home.earthlink.net/~mikeq/randam/

A fun rubber stamp kit for you to make your own red rubber stamps:

Artisan's Choice

2066 Wineridge Place

Escondido, CA 92029

(877) 727-8472

www.artisanschoice.com

⊚ Magazines

Expression
P.O. Box 16025
San Diego, CA 92176-9985
www.expressionartmagazine.com

The Rubber Gazette
P.O. Box 215
Pascoe Vale South VIC 3044
Australia

The Rubber Stamper
(published by Hobby Publications, Inc.)
P.O. Box 102
Morganville, NJ 07751-0102
(800) 260-9028
www.rubberstamper.com

RubberStampMadness
P.O. Box 610
Corvallis, OR 97339-0610
(877) STAMPMA
www.rsmadness.com

Stamping Arts & Crafts
(published by Scott Publications)
30595 Eight Mile
Livonia, MI 48152
(800) 458-8237
http://66.96.222.139/sacmag/

Stampington & Company
22992 Mill Creek, Ste. B
Laguna Hills, CA 92653
(877) STAMPER
www.stampington.com
▪ *publisher of* Belle Armoire, Somerset Studio,
Stamper's Sampler *and* Stampington Inspirations

The Studio Zine
(Teesha Moore)
P.O. Box 3329
Renton, WA 98056
www.thestudiozine.com

Vamp Stamp News
P.O. Box 386
Hanover, MD 21076-0386
(410) 760-3377
www.vampstampnews.com

⊚ Author Contact Info

Gains & McCall
P.O. Box 4901
Covina, CA 91723
www.gainsandmccall.com

INDEX

EXPLORE THE EXCITING WORLD OF *rubber stamps* with NORTH LIGHT BOOKS!

Discover great new tricks for creating extra-special greeting cards! Pick up your stamp, follow along with the illustrated, step-by-step directions inside, and ta da!—you'll amaze everyone (including yourself!) with your beautiful and original creations.

ISBN 0-89134-979-0, paperback, 128 pages, #31521-K

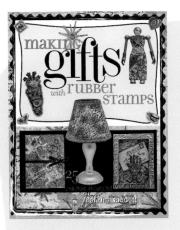

Use your favorite rubber stamps to create 25 gorgeous gifts and miniature works of art! Inside you'll find dozens of simple methods for creating sophisticated embellishments on everything from lampshades and pushpins to adorable mini shadow boxes and handmade books.

ISBN 1-58180-081-9, paperback, 128 pages, #31667-K

Here are hundreds of colorful ideas and techniques for creating one-of-a-kind greetings—from the elegant to the festive to the downright goofy—all in a matter of minutes! Try your hand at any of the 30 step-by-step projects inside or take off in your own original direction.

ISBN 0-89134-713-5, paperback, 128 pages, #30821-K

Use rubber stamps to decorate candles, jewelry, purses, book covers, wall hangings and more. Sixteen step-by-step projects show you how by using creative techniques, surfaces and embellishments, including metal, beads, embossing powder and clay—even shrink plastic!

ISBN 1-58180-128-9, paperback, 128 pages, #31829-K

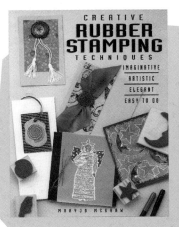

Learn how to create fancier greeting cards, cooler note cards and prettier invitations with MaryJo McGraw's easy-to-master methods. Inside you'll find more than 30 fast and fun step-by-step projects that mix and match techniques for truly original results!

ISBN 0-89134-878-6, paperback, 128 pages, #31201-K

THESE BOOKS and other fine North Light titles are available from your local art & craft retailer, bookstore, online supplier or by calling 1-800-448-0915.